1 Stepin Fetchit
2 Fred Astaire
3 William Powell
4 Myrna Loy
5 Vivien Leigh
6 Laurence Olivier
7 Raimu
8 Michel Simon
9 Gina Lollobrigida
10 Adolphe Menjou
11 Spencer Tracy
12 Clark Gable
13 John Gilbert
14 John Barrymore
15 Fernandel
16 Boris Karloff
17 Louis Jouvet
18 Michele Morgan
19 Charles Boyer
20 Warner Oland
21 Lon Chaney
22 Charles Laughton
23 Edward G. Robinson
24 Peter Lorre
25 Bela Lugosi
26 Joan Crawford
27 Jean Gabin
28 Alec Guinness
29 Anna Magnani
30 Maurice Chevalier
31 Erich von Stroheim
32 Jean Harlow
33 Rudolph Valentino
34 Bette Davis
35 Greta Garbo
36 Rita Hayworth
37 Theda Bara
38 Marlene Dietrich
39 Hedy Lamarr
40 Mae West
41 Gerard Philipe
42 Mickey Mouse
43 Harpo Marx
44 Groucho Marx
45 Chico Marx
46 Wallace Beery
47 Marie Dressler
48 Orson Welles
49 George Arliss
50 Marilyn Monroe
51 Charlie Chaplin
52 Buster Keaton
53 Oliver Hardy
54 Stan Laurel
55 Mickey Rooney
56 W. C. Fields
57 Bing Crosby
58 Judy Garland
59 Bob Hope
60 Harry Langdon
61 Harold Lloyd
62 Clara Bow
63 Ben Turpin
64 William S. Hart
65 Jimmy Durante
66 Ingrid Bergman
67 Gary Cooper
68 Lillian Gish
69 Dorothy Gish
70 Gloria Swanson
71 Mary Pickford
72 Douglas Fairbanks
73 Katharine Hepburn
74 Norma Shearer
75 Shirley Temple

The endpapers by Al Hirschfeld, for which this diagram is the key, originally appeared in LIFE's issue of May 17, 1954.

LIFE LIFE LIFE GOES TO THE MOVIES

TIME-LIFE BOOKS, INC.
ALEXANDRIA, VIRGINIA

TIME-LIFE BOOKS
FOUNDER: Henry R. Luce 1898-1967

LIFE GOES TO THE MOVIES

EDITOR: David E. Scherman
Designer: Thomas S. Huestis
Text editor: Frank K. Kappler
Staff Writers: Richard Cravens, Richard Oulahan,
James A. Randall, Jill Spiller
Researchers: Joyce Pelto, Fran Ahders,
Thomas Fitzharris, Judith Greene, Ruth Kelton,
Thomas Lashnits, Brian McGinn,
Mary Carroll Marden, Gabrielle Smith
Design Assistant: Deanna Lorenz
Film Consultant and Design Assistant:
Lou Valentino
Editorial Assistant: Wendy Karsten

Editorial Production
Production Editor: Douglas B. Graham
Assistant Production Editors:
Gennaro C. Esposito, Feliciano Madrid
Quality Director: Robert L. Young
Assistant Quality Director: James J. Cox
Associate: Serafino J. Cambareri
Copy Staff: Eleanore W. Karsten (chief),
Mary Orlando, Charles Blackwell,
Susan B. Galloway, Georgia Ingersoll,
Florence Keith, Pearl Sverdlin
Picture Department: Dolores A. Littles,
Martin Baldessari
Traffic: Carmen McLellan

The editors were greatly aided by former LIFE staff
members Sean Callahan, Judy Fayard, Stanley
Flink, John Frook, Dora Jane Hamblin, Philip
Kunhardt, James Lebenthal, Richard Pollard,
Richard Schickel, Richard B. Stolley, Thomas
Thompson, Loudon Wainwright and David Zeitlin.

Valuable assistance was provided by the following
departments and individuals of Time Inc.: Editorial
Production, Norman Airey; Library, Benjamin
Lightman; Picture Collection, Doris O'Neil;
Photographic Laboratory, George Karas, Herb Orth,
Renate Haarhoff; Time Inc. Archives, Lillian Owens;
TIME-LIFE News Service, Murray J. Gart;
Correspondents Maria Vincenza Aloisi (Paris), Lois
Armstrong (Los Angeles), Margot Hapgood
(London), Villette Harris (Washington, D.C.), Ann
Natanson (Rome), Sue Wymelenberg (Boston).

ISBN 0-517-62585-7

h g f e d c b a

Contents

Love Story

by TOM PRIDEAUX

This book is about a magazine's love affair with an industry.

From the start, LIFE and the movies were hooked by each other, behaving by turns like partners or rivals, soul mates or outraged enemies. All of us who worked for the magazine —especially those of us in the Entertainment section—were caught up in the relationship. The strongest common bond, of course, was photography. But temperamentally, too, we at LIFE and they in Hollywood were pretty much alike, racing to meet production deadlines, enjoying our work—and even the overwork. Through the years—plying each other with sweet talk and champagne, or slamming doors in each other's faces—we had an absolutely wonderful time together.

During LIFE's span, from 1936 to 1972, the Movie Department filled more pages than any other editorial beat except the focal Newsfronts section. Many issues contained two or more movie stories; and of the total of 1,864 covers, more than 250 were devoted to film stars, or incipient stars. Yet, despite this massive attention, the magazine's Hollywood coverage remained incorrigibly personal, dictated mainly by the enthusiasms, the hunches and the crotchets of editors, photographers and reporters. Because a need for access and cooperation forced us repeatedly to torment the same film companies, the same stars, the same press agents, we came to regard one another—if not always with equal affection— as kindred tribesmen. With the probable exception of the magazine's war correspondents, no other groups within the staff felt more fervently dedicated to their jobs.

All this is reflected in the book you are now holding in your hands. It is by no means a systematic, conscientious history of Hollywood; you will not find in it all of your favorite movies or stars, or even all of the movies and performers that LIFE gave room to. Limitations of

During his 34 years at LIFE, Tom Prideaux was variously its Movie Editor and Entertainment Editor—and one of the nation's leading drama critics.

space alone, even in so large a volume, would have made that impossible. Furthermore, other valuable books about the movies are available to serve the historical record.

We have chosen, instead, to winnow from the finest pictures in LIFE's files more than 750 selections, which recapture both the symbiosis between reporters and reportees and the art that the magazine itself brought to its photographic coverage of moviemaking. It should also be pointed out that there is more here than the Hollywood of LIFE's lifetime: even though LIFE did not begin publication until the mid-'30s, it printed, through the ensuing years, many rare old pictures documenting early film history. The best of that vintage are also in this volume.

"Movie of the Week," which used stills to report on new releases, appeared in issue No. 2 and was the magazine's first regular movie feature. Usually the studios provided these pictures, which were shot for publicity purposes by their own photographers. The editors took their pick and fitted the selections into layouts with captions and critical comments. Even when nothing very nice was said, the producers considered it an honor to have been chosen for attention; thus, many a film was heavily advertised with the headline "LIFE's Movie of the Week," as if its selection was an automatic accolade.

In addition to this feature, the Entertainment staff soon began to explore the film community itself—its stars, its ways of working and playing. And the result was the real beginning of the big romance. While much of it was conducted in Los Angeles, where the magazine maintained its principal West Coast bureau, it ultimately became a global affair, springing up in Rome, Madrid, Paris, Tahiti, London —wherever there were actors and cameras.

In the long succession of far-flung editors who worked LIFE's movie beat, one—Mary Leatherbee—stands out particularly. In ways that cannot be measured by those who did not know her, this book belongs to Mary. She

Peter Stackpole caught Ginger Rogers as Kitty Foyle.

Chili Williams, surprise pin-up queen, was never a star.

Mary Leatherbee (1910-1972) conceived LIFE's most imaginative coverage of Hollywood.

joined the staff in 1945 after serving in World War II as a bomber ferry pilot. All during the 27 years of her involvement she was never content merely to observe and react to the assignments she dreamed up; she was driven to participate personally. For example, when Cecil B. De Mille was shooting parts of *The Greatest Show on Earth* (1952) at the Ringling Brothers-Barnum & Bailey Circus winter quarters in Sarasota, Mary took it as a matter of course that she could get the full flavor of the story only by rehearsing personally with 26 girl acrobats and being hoisted aloft on ropes for the aerial ballet. For the filming of Walt Disney's *20,000 Leagues Under the Sea* (1954), three miles off Nassau, Mary strapped an aqualung on her back for the first time and made a dozen plunges to the ocean floor to monitor the shooting of Captain Nemo's underwater funeral.

Mary could switch instantly from grave concern to laughter; and her shifting moods —teasing, scolding or acting out funny stories —always energized the ozone. But more than that, her undisguised honesty won her the trust and confidence of Hollywood's biggest names; they cooperated on almost anything she phoned to suggest, and warmed noticeably to their chores if she showed up herself.

It was under Mary's editorship that LIFE recruited the unprecedented array of stars who appeared in the special acts she dreamed up for two of the magazine's most successful and memorable year-end issues: those of 1958 and 1963. For the first of these she concocted an oldtime Mack Sennett comedy, swarming with Keystone Cops and bathing beauties, played by such stars as Kim Novak, Lee Remick, Debbie Reynolds and Rock Hudson. She also persuaded Marilyn Monroe to dress up and pose for a gallery of old entertainment stars such as Lillian Russell, Theda Bara and Jean Harlow. For the 1963 issue, she produced a nostalgic album of typical scenes from early movies with a blockbuster modern cast: Bing Crosby, Tony Curtis, Cary Grant, Audrey Hepburn, Bob Hope, Jack Lemmon,

Shirley MacLaine, Paul Newman, Frank Sinatra and Natalie Wood *(pages 256-257).*

Such cooperation was all the more remarkable because the stars were justifiably wary. They knew that stories planned for any issue were often scratched at the last minute to make room for more urgent editorial material. But even though forewarned, they were invariably hurt and often angry when the acts for which they had put themselves out were dropped. Clark Gable, after spending a week at a ranch posing for a layout that was never used, damned LIFE to hell and swore never to collaborate again. It was nearly 10 years before he agreed to give us another chance at him. (This time the story ran; part of it appears on page 130.)

After 16 years, LIFE discontinued "Movie of the Week" and began to invade the sound stages—shooting important scenes over the director's shoulder and often being a terrible nuisance. Gradually, though, our assigned photographers were fitted into filming schedules, usually at previously specified times during the day's work.

After a while the producers, having recovered from the shock of seeing how intensely and imaginatively our photographers applied themselves, wanted to hire them to shoot their publicity stills. A refusal on the editors' part could have meant a narrowing of studio access. As a result, many compromise deals were worked out. Sam Goldwyn, for example, paid Gjon Mili to shoot the stills for *Guys and Dolls* (1955), knowing that LIFE would have first choice among the resulting pictures. On the other hand, Eliot Elisofon was signed up by John Huston not as a still photographer at all but as a color consultant for *Moulin Rouge (page 179),* Huston's glowing biography of the artist Toulouse-Lautrec.

The possibility that the magazine could influence the studios had become evident early when editor Daniel Longwell heard of RKO's plans to make a movie of Christopher Morley's best-selling novel *Kitty Foyle* (1940).

Gordon Parks "scalps" his subject, dancer Diane Sinclair.

Jumping the gun, the editors staged key sequences in the book's narrative, had them photographed, published the results as "research notes" for the yet-to-be-made film —and later commented in print, with great satisfaction, that the completed motion picture, with Ginger Rogers' Oscar-winning performance as Kitty, hewed remarkably close to the original LIFE treatment.

A similar project was photographer John Florea's still-picture version of Franz Werfel's novel, *The Song of Bernadette.* Johnny used as the young heroine nun the as-yet-unknown actress Jennifer Jones, who had just been signed as the lead. When the film went into production, he visited the set and found Henry King directing a scene while holding the LIFE issue containing the story. "Thanks," King said, "for doing my work for me."

Altogether, LIFE published a dozen such stories, including David Scherman's treatment of Eric Knight's novel, *This Above All,* later filmed with Tyrone Power (1942); and a suggested treatment for Ernest Hemingway's *For Whom the Bell Tolls* in 1941, in which the editors used Robert Capa's Spanish Civil War photos and even recommended Gary Cooper and Ingrid Bergman for the leading roles. One staff member, D. M. Marshman Jr., found a particularly profitable way to influence Hollywood. During a visit there he was invited by the writing team of Charles Brackett and Billy Wilder to a screening of their unreleased film, *The Emperor Waltz* (1948). When they asked for his opinion, he criticized it in such impressive terms that they invited him to collaborate with them on a future movie. He did. The result was the Academy Award winner *Sunset*

For 36 years, LIFE went to the movies through the eyes of these photographers: Carlo Bavagnoli, John Bryson, Edward Clark, Ralph Crane, Loomis Dean, John Dominis, Paul Dorsey, Alfred Eisenstaedt, Eliot Elisofon, Bill Eppridge, J. R. Eyerman, N. R. Farbman, John Florea, Herbert Gehr, Allan Grant, Milton H. Greene, Philippe Halsman, Marie Hansen, Rex Hardy Jr., Martha Holmes, Mark Kauffman, Bob Landry, John Loengard, Gjon Mili, Leonard McCombe, Gordon Parks, Bill Ray, Mike Rougier, Walt Sanders, Arthur Schatz, W. Eugene Smith, Terry Spencer and Peter Stackpole.

Eliot Elisofon joins Alfred Hitchcock at work on a projec

Allan Grant shines in spotlighted Audrey Hepburn's reflectio

Stackpole slips himself into a shot of Carole Landis and fan.

Ed Clark sets up shop cheek by jowl with a cinematographe

John Florea coaches a "nun" for his version of Bernadette.

Leonard McCombe directs Kim Novak for his own LIFE ac

n Mili gets a free ride from Marlon Brando on the Guys and Dolls set.

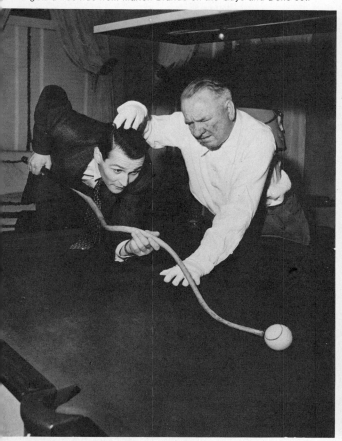

ph Crane, with a twisted cue, learns about pool from W. C. Fields.

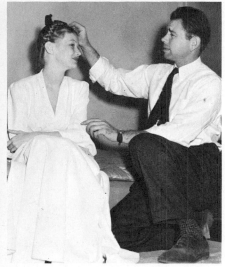

Bob Landry fluffs Veronica Lake's famed hair.

Philippe Halsman aims for one of his 101 covers.

Martha Holmes rides the boom at a musical.

Alfred Eisenstaedt chortles over Sophia's infant.

Boulevard (1950), starring Gloria Swanson.

What was it really worth to a young star to be pictured in LIFE? No one really knew, but there were estimates in the early days that a LIFE cover appearance might add as much as a million dollars to a star's career income. Slowly that theory was eroded by incontrovertible fact: as the years passed, lots of pretty girls appeared in the magazine—and on its cover—and then simply vanished from sight.

If any doubt remained, the case of Chili Williams, the Polka-Dot Girl, settled the question. In 1943, model magnate Harry Conover submitted a picture of a laughing, wind-blown blonde, holding a prop oar and wearing an eye-catching two-piece swimsuit with large polka dots. It was printed, small, in a catch-all department, "Pictures to the Editors," along with Conover's letter, which said: "Sirs: This picture shows Miss Chili Williams, my newest cover girl. I think she has all the photogenic qualities which have brought fame to other Cover Girls, including Choo Choo Johnson, Candy Jones, Dusty Anderson, Anita Colby. This is one of her first pictures."

Overnight, letters poured in from readers, asking for another—larger—look. The editors cooperated; Chili appeared twice more and as a result received, it was said, some 100,000 fan letters. She was grabbed by Hollywood; clearly, she was destined for great things. Time passed. Chili had a bit part or two—and then quietly disappeared into oblivion, along with all estimates of the high monetary value of exposure in LIFE's pages.

In just about all other respects, however, the love affair between LIFE and the movies proved to be valuable indeed. Yes, it was enormously useful for the studios in promoting their products. Yes, it was wonderfully effective for the editors in brightening the magazine's pages. But the chief beneficiaries of this long-running romance were LIFE's readers, who were treated week after week to a banquet almost as rich and frothy as the Hollywood product itself. The flavor lingers on, and is recaptured in the pages that follow.

*Master merchandising gimmick of the big studios,
Hollywood's Star System elevated ordinary mortals to
demigods, hoisting them with the leverage created
by myths and money. For a fledgling picture magazine, it
was a heavenly opportunity to have great fun.*

The Stars

When the new magazine LIFE appeared on the scene in 1936, pledged, among other things, "to see life—to see and be amazed," Garbo had lost her first name, Shirley Temple was Queen of the box office and Clark Gable was King. The Star System was flourishing. Exploiting it, the masters of the big studios heavily promoted their contract-bound performers, whose followers raised them to the status of popular deities. The resulting Star System was either the greatest boon or the greatest bane of the movies, depending on who was talking. To the industry, and to most of the millions of fans who bought 88 million tickets each week, it was the means by which the greatest entertainment medium ever devised fulfilled itself, outrivaling the Greeks in its outpouring of tragedy and comedy. To some critics it was the death of art. To LIFE it was something to ponder philosophically, to criticize artistically and to recall nostalgically when it yielded, in the 1960s, to the era of the TV-movie and the star-controlled "movie movie." But all that was later. Right off the bat, LIFE embraced the system.

Not only could it use all the stars there were; it would manufacture new ones. Richard Pollard, an early LIFE movie correspondent, recalled in later years how he and Peter Stackpole—the staff photographer whose early candid pictures of Hollywood starlets were to the ordinary studio handout as The Last Supper is to a plumbing company's Christmas calendar—discovered a well-endowed San Bernardino dancer named Frances Lillian Mary Ridste. She had changed her name to Carole Landis and won a part as a kempt cave woman in Hal Roach's *One Million B.C.* "We published the first of Stackpole's pictures," Pollard said, "and Carole's salary went from $75 a week to $750 a week. Peter did another story a year later and she was raised to $2,500 a week. She called to thank me and asked what she could do in gratitude. I said I'd always wanted a Swiss Army knife."

In the '40s, war and postwar problems muted that kind of nuttiness. The decade also carried the seeds of change in LIFE's relationship to the stars. As LIFE movie critic Richard Schickel later wrote in his book *The Stars,* the early years of sound, giving voices to the screen's heroes and heroines, had reduced them from silent, inscrutable gods to beings who resembled, more or less, real people. By the '50s, covering them as mere mortals was a substantial challenge, and one not without responsibilities.

In 1952, Marilyn Monroe was doing bit parts for 20th Century-Fox. While appearing in a small role in *Don't Bother To Knock,* she went to Stanley Flink, a LIFE movie reporter and a good friend, with a worrisome problem. Three years before, broke, she had modeled in the nude for a calendar photograph, and she had now been spotted as its subject. A studio executive had told her she should disown it or face ruin. Flink, aware that the wire services already had the story, said to her, "Just tell us the whole truth and trust us." He wired New York, which was at work on its first major story about Marilyn as a frequently publicized starlet, and suggested that the article should include Marilyn's calendar misadventure, decorously downplayed. The editors agreed, and a Philippe Halsman photograph of Marilyn made the cover —and history *(page 64).* The story, headlined "Hollywood Topic A-Plus," included a tiny reproduction of the calendar picture and these words: "She even posed for calendar art for a few badly needed extra pennies." The story created a sensation, but it also won a sympathetic response. Marilyn, weeping, told Flink it had saved her life.

Sometimes that same sense of responsibility caused the editors to tone down a naturally sensational story. While they were preparing to close a picture act about Clark Gable at work on *The Misfits* in 1960 *(page 41),* he suffered a severe heart attack at his home. Hollywood correspondent David Zeitlin—whose industry sources, his colleagues knew, were impeccable—told New York The King's days were numbered, though Gable himself did not know it. Rather than publish that headline-making fact and deal a possible psychological blow to Gable, the editors, who knew he was looking forward to the issue, minimized the seriousness of his illness. Moreover, they wrote that a decision Gable had made the day before his coronary, to cancel a planned visit to his remote hunting lodge, had perhaps "saved his life. Had he been far from medical care, the attack could have killed him."

And so, for three and a half decades, LIFE kept the stars close to its heart and on its covers. It ran stories on matinee idols, sex symbols, girl-next-door types, tough-guy types, beauties from abroad and the new breed of purposeful actors. Some waxed, waned and died before LIFE itself was spent. One movie immortal was already an old-timer when LIFE began; but she was still a star of the brightest magnitude —and more beautiful than ever—when she dropped by the New York office "to help" ready a story about her that was scheduled to run in that week's issue. At 4 p.m. the editor sent out for champagne, assuring her that such a break was routine at that hour. Next day two bottles of the best were delivered precisely on time. The accompanying note read: "It's 4 o'clock. Marlene." That was LIFE among The Stars.

*Eleven of Hollywood's most durable performers grace
just nine of the 290 covers that LIFE devoted to movie
stars during its 36-year publishing history.*

LIFE

AFTER A BOUT
WITH CANCER
John Wayne
is back in action

MAY 7 · 1965 · 35¢

LIFE

MRS. ERNEST HEMINGWAY'S
SENTIMENTAL SAFARI

CLEOPATRA Most Talked
About Movie Ever Made

RICHARD BURTON
LIZ TAYLOR

APRIL 19 · 1963 · 25¢

LIFE

BOMB TESTS: Struggle of Conscience
MOMENTOUS DECISION
FACING THE PRESIDENT
Powers–Abel Album

ALSO THIS WEEK

5 & 10 Man's Grand Gift:
$50 Million in Art
to Our Towns and Cities

Fashion Switch—
Little Girls' Styles
Capture Grownups

Easygoing Rock
in Another Hit

ROCK
HUDSON

FEBRUARY 16 · 1962 · 20¢

LIFE

KATHARINE HEPBURN

JANUARY 6, 1941 **10** CENTS

LIFE

TIGER-EYED
TEMPTRESS,
SOPHIA LOREN

NOVEMBER 14, 1960

LIFE

INGRID BERGMAN

NOVEMBER 12, 1945 **10** CENTS

LIFE

ASTAIRE & ROGERS DO THE YAM

AUGUST 22, 1938 **10** CENTS

LIFE

Gable's
Last Film

JANUARY 13, 1961

LIFE

JUDY GARLAND

DECEMBER 11, 1944 **10** CENTS

The Heroines

Hundreds of female stars were discovered, covered and uncovered during LIFE's lifetime. Some of them were quite special—and a treasured few were one-of-a-kind.

They were a legendary lot: Judy, Ingrid, Liz, Marilyn, Sophia—to name a few. But there were four who, through six generations of editors, probably won and retained the highest professional esteem of them all: Garbo and Dietrich, Davis and Hepburn.

The most photogenic face in movie history had already made a millionaire of Greta Gustafsson before there was a magazine called LIFE. She was featured in the first issue, dated November 23, 1936. That was 11 years after the Swedish director Mauritz Stiller had brought her to the United States, and she was being paid $250,000 to $300,000 a picture. An acknowledged superstar (although the term had not yet been invented), she was billed by Metro-Goldwyn-Mayer simply as Garbo, the stage name Stiller had contrived by rearranging the letters in Gabor, the name of a Hungarian king. But the Garbo legend of the reclusive, parsimonious queen of the cinèma was still growing. LIFE delighted in it and pursued it even after Garbo retired in 1941.

The name invariably linked to Garbo's in the Hollywood pantheon of glamor goddesses is that of Marlene (a diminutive of Maria Magdalena) Dietrich, another exotic European import of pre-LIFE days, who became filmdom's longest-running myth. Marlene, the Berlin-born daughter of a Prussian lancer who died when she was a child, learned French and English from governesses, prepared for a concert violinist's career, gave it up at about 18 for drama school, played minor roles in a number of German movies and was appearing in a Berlin satirical review when Josef von Sternberg spotted the Dietrich legs and signed her to display them and her then voluptuous figure in *The Blue Angel.* She played a cabaret singer who drove Emil Jannings into lustful paroxysms with her sultry rendition of

"Falling in Love Again." Von Sternberg brought her to the United States and, aided by Paramount's publicity platoons, built her up as the embodiment of the foreign siren —meanwhile slimming her down to compete with Garbo. When she made *Knight Without Armor* in 1937, the brand-new magazine reported, London Films paid her $450,000, making her the highest-paid woman in the world.

Bette Davis and Katharine Hepburn were two quirky New England individualists who refused to conform to Hollywood's idea of how stars should act but went on anyhow to become two of the most respected actresses in film history. Out of Massachusetts, Bette Davis came to Hollywood in 1930, "trailing clouds of obscurity," as LIFE subsequently put it. No one met her at the railroad station because she didn't look like an actress and the studio press agent failed to recognize her. By the time LIFE ceased publication she had made more than 80 pictures, won 10 Oscar nominations and two Oscars.

Hepburn did even better. A Connecticut surgeon's daughter who as a child had accompanied her mother on women's-suffrage campaigns, Hepburn was an instant success in her first film, *A Bill of Divorcement* (1932). Typically, although she had been tested originally because of the lissome legs she displayed on the stage as an Amazon in *The Warrior's Husband,* she persisted in wearing slacks simply because she found them comfortable. In her third film, *Morning Glory,* in 1933, she won her first Oscar and thereafter never let up. By 1972 she had made close to 40 movies and added a second, then an unprecedented third Oscar—for *Guess Who's Coming to Dinner* (1967) and *The Lion in Winter* (1968). Altogether, she received 11 Academy nominations—one more even than Davis.

In a three-part series of articles on Garbo in 1955, LIFE described her real romance with John Gilbert and the superheated lovemaking it had inspired in the silent film Flesh and the Devil, made in 1927.

11

Greta Garbo

At first the former lather girl from a Stockholm barber shop was ignored by M-G-M's moguls. But they finally looked again at that face, made for the camera.

A compliant Garbo and resentful leading man Antonio Moreno take direction from the domineering Mauritz Stiller in The Temptress (1926). LIFE, in a 1955 series on the star, described Stiller as ''A Hypnotic Director'' who ''Made Over Even Her Very Soul.'' Replaced, he returned to Sweden and shortly died.

Garbo, already a star at home, was heading back to ▶ Sweden when Stiller showed M-G-M executives this and other photographs, made by Arnold Genthe, that captured the marvelous plasticity of her features. ''It was hard to believe the pictures he took were all of the same girl,'' wrote John Bainbridge.

In Ninotchka (1939), when Garbo laughed in her first comedy, the ads plugged it as the biggest news since she first spoke in Anna Christie (1930).

Marlene Dietrich

Another glamorous import outlasted Garbo, parlaying sensational legs, photogenic cheekbones and a throaty voice into the longest-running myth in movie history.

Ferns in her hair and water dripping over the fam[...] planes of her face, Marlene Dietrich managed to lo[...] sizzling even after a plunge into a forest pool. T[...] scene is a still from 1937's Knight Without Armor.

She was four years into her new career as the world's sexiest grandmother when Milton H. Greene took this unforgettable photograph of Dietrich in 1952.

The celebrated legs won their first U.S. exposure in the German film The Blue Angel (1930). "It was Dietrich's gift," LIFE observed in 1938, "to invest with glamor the role of a thinly disguised harlot."

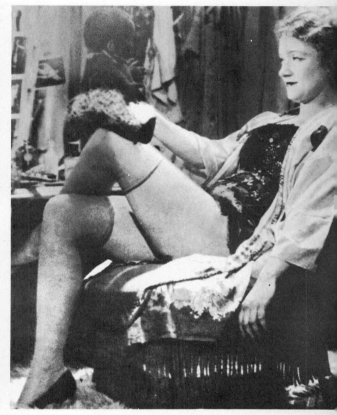

In 1957 Marlene's mystique still held up superbly. Officially 53, she starred in Billy Wilder's adaptation of Agatha Christie's Witness for the Prosecution.

Bette Davis

Studios decided that the big-eyed New Englander was unsexy, but in four decades of roles that accented assorted disasters, she outgrossed many a sex bomb.

For What Ever Happened to Baby Jane? (1962), a latter-day horror film that co-starred Joan Crawford, Bette designed and applied her own macabre make-up. In the course of her distinguished movie career, LIFE observed, she endured more misfortune and suffering than any other woman in screen history.

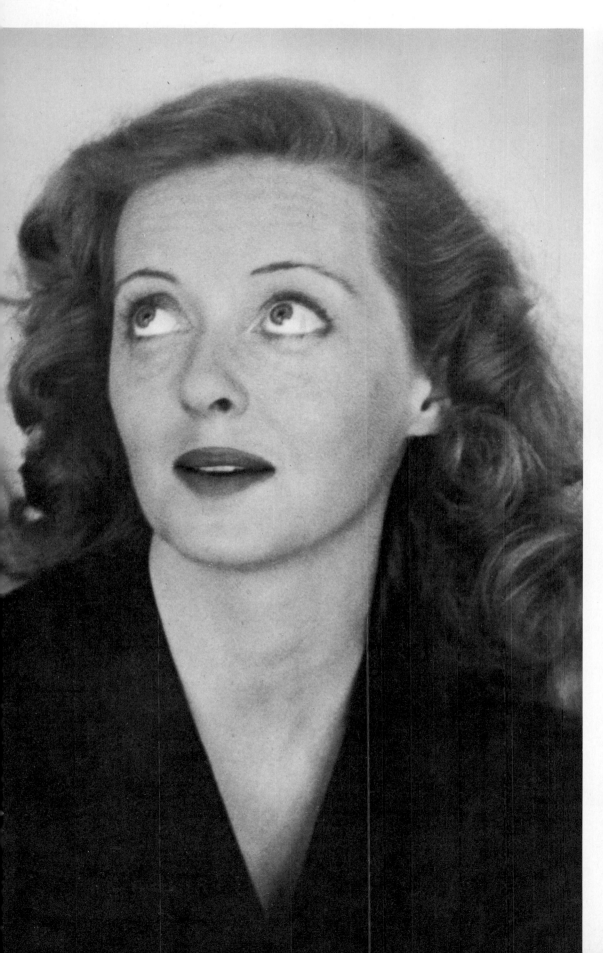

In 1941, LIFE went to Bette's 33rd-birthday party at her usually very private house in New Hampshire. Just back from the ski slope, she had turned off the electricity that charged her public personality.

Bette's 1939 cover portrait almost destroyed her determinedly nonglamorous image. Producer Carl Laemmle Jr. had said on viewing her 1930 screen tests: "That gal has about as much sex appeal as Slim Summerville." When this picture was made, Bette had her two Oscars and was Warners' top star.

Katharine Hepburn

On screen and off, from the outset she was an original: a fierce individualist who flouted some of Hollywood's most hallowed conventions during an incomparable career.

Woman of the Year (1942) was the first of nine films Hepburn and Spencer Tracy did together. Through the years, LIFE often took note of their "close friendship," but never reported their touching love story.

Asked to sit for this cover picture when she was rehearsing in London for the filming of The Lion in Winter (1968), the 58-year-old actress showed up in a typical Hepburn costume and struck a typical Hepburn pose, with the smile she described to photographer Terry Spencer as her "Girl Scout look."

Katharine Hepburn, who may have been the single greatest influence in popularizing slacks for women, returned to Broadway in 1950 as Rosalind in Shakespeare's As You Like It. After her seven-year absence, LIFE discovered to its surprise and delight that "her gams were as good as her iambics."

Wearing a strip of burlap as a headdress to get the feel of her costume, Hepburn plays the 1968 Lion in Winter role of Eleanor of Aquitaine, the part that won her a third Oscar. As the magazine had previously noted, "When Katharine Hepburn sets out to play Katharine Hepburn, nobody is her equal."

Shirley Temple

America's dimpled sweetheart stole movies from just about everybody during a mini-career that put her among the top 10 box-office stars from 1934 through 1939.

Fifty-five golden curls bouncing on her adorable little head, Shirley Temple was far and away the most popular child star ever. Between the ages of 4 and 13, she tapped, sang and lit up the screen through 30 movies. The warmth she radiated with her dimpled grin and mock-heroic strut were in happy contrast to the cold, gray times. They set off a Temple craze that resulted in the sale of millions of Shirley milk mugs, Shirley dolls, Shirley hats, Shirley dresses, Shirley soap and even Shirley underwear. In 1937 LIFE called her "a fitting symbol of Hollywood." "She is young," the new magazine said, "and Hollywood is the place where the very young are made very famous faster than anywhere else on earth."

Kid stars had been around before Shirley and they continued turning up after she stepped aside: Jackie Coogan and Jackie Cooper in the 1920s and '30s; Mickey Rooney, Judy Garland and Deanna Durbin in the '30s and '40s; Brandon De Wilde in the '50s. But Shirley had something more than the cuteness that makes adorable tots the bane of grown-up actors. She was also a talented dancer and singer who was not just a foil but a match for performers like Bill "Bojangles" Robinson and George Murphy.

Despite her charm and sparkle, Shirley's screen popularity, like that of most film children, didn't really survive her little girlhood. Studio tom-toms beat hard to stir up interest in the maturing Shirley; LIFE ran a cover story on her in 1940, when she had just turned 12, showing her as a pretty, rather serious pre-teenager, but all to no avail. America's baby sweetheart was really over the celluloid hill.

In 1937 at the peak of her unprecedented popularity, Shirley Temple found time to play croquet. Just 9 years old, she was earning $300,000 a year.

Shirley at 3, as a scrubwoman in Baby Burlesks (1931)

Eyed by Adolph Menjou in 1934's Little Miss Marker

Dancing with Bill Robinson in The Littlest Rebel (1935)

A crinolined dream-sequence princess in Heidi (1937)

On a Washington visit, a kiss for J. Edgar Hoover

With George Murphy in Little Miss Broadway (1938)

A lanky, cavorting 12-year-old in Young People (1940)

At an on-set celebration for her 16th birthday in 1944

With her bridegroom, Sergeant John Agar, in 1945

Shirley with her daughter Lori, 3, on a 1958 LIFE cover

Ingrid Bergman

*This fresh-faced Swede, touted as a young Garbo,
developed a personal style and a commanding presence
that withstood the periodic eclipses of her U.S. career.*

In 1941, less than two years after her arrival in the U.S., LIFE called Bergman "Sweden's most promising export since Greta Garbo." Here, she enjoys a skiing vacation in California. After leaving Hollywood in 1949, she made no U.S. films at all for seven years, then appeared only in U.S. movies made abroad.

Ernest Hemingway saw Bergman in her first U.S. picture, Intermezzo, and asked her to accept the role of the Spanish guerrilla Maria in For Whom the Bell Tolls. "If you don't act in the picture, Ingrid," he said, "I won't work on it." Bergman did, and shared that famous sleeping bag with Gary Cooper.

When liberated Ingrid Bergman left child and husband in 1949 to join Italian director Roberto Rossellini, scandalized fans boycotted her pictures. After 18 years' self-exile in Europe she returned to play in O'Neill's More Stately Mansions, and was visited in her dressing room by Pia Lindstrom, her look-alike daughter.

Audrey Hepburn

A slip of an ex-ballerina with the melting eyes of a gazelle charmed LIFE's editors, who followed her career in almost as many cover stories as they gave Liz, Marilyn and Sophia.

In her six covers Audrey appeared

"Horsing around," as LIFE put it, Audrey did something for a white wool suit by Hubert de Givenchy in a 1962 story. The excuse for coverage was her affinity for the fashions of Givenchy, whose rise to eminence in his field coincided with her own in films.

Robed as the nurse heroine of The Nun's Story (1959), Audrey ignores kibitzing crowned cranes and reads while on location in Africa. Director Billy Wilder told LIFE the bright, Dutch-born ex-ballerina "gives the distinct impression she can spell schizophrenia."

...he phone, renting a villa near Rome, as Natasha in War and Peace, with husband Mel Ferrer in a television version of Mayerling, in The Nun's Story, and modeling a spring hat.

Judy Garland

A trouper who had never known real childhood sang away her adolescence and her youth as well, en route to an extraordinary niche in the entertainment world.

Fatigued by the endless retakes her perfectionism demanded, Judy Garland rests on the set of A Star Is Born (1954), in which she came back after four years of film blackout and personal turmoil. Fired after 11 years' intense productivity, she had tried suicide and worsened her drug problem with alcohol.

Born Frances Ethel Gumm and schooled on the M-G-M lot, Judy grew up to fulfill her boundless talents in Meet Me in St. Louis (1944) in what LIFE called "her handsomest role since The Wizard of Oz."

At 17, Judy got the plum role as the little farm girl in The Wizard of Oz because Shirley Temple was unavailable. Garland was born in 1922, two years later made her stage debut at the theater in Grand Rapids, Minn., run by her ex-vaudevillian parents.

Told in 1959 that she would never work again, a determinedly convalescent Judy prepared for another of many comebacks—a 1961 concert tour that drew adoring crowds. Of this portrait, LIFE said, "Judy reflects the courage she gained from her triumph over the past." She was 47 when she died in 1969.

Elizabeth Taylor

An angelic child became LIFE's champion cover girl while managing to acquire a pair of Oscars, five husbands, four children and the most public private life in the world.

As depicted on 11 covers in 25 year

When LIFE ran this Toni Frissell portrait of Elizabeth and Mike Todd with their new baby, Elizabeth (called Liza), in 1957, mamma Liz already had two sons by her previous husband, Michael Wilding.

Elizabeth Taylor's life unfolded like a soap opera: the pretty youngster grew up to become a beautiful and talented woman of the world who was beset by marital and physical woes.

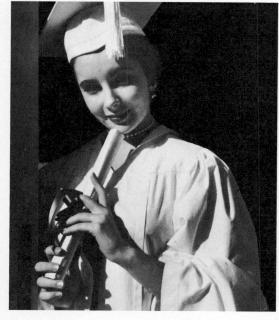

After eight years' study at the M-G-M studio school, Elizabeth got her diploma from Hollywood's University High. LIFE reported that she had earned a B-plus average and shown "a flair for writing."

Shortly before turning 17, a year before she received her diploma, Elizabeth sat for photographer Philippe Halsman in a decolleté evening dress of gold silk.

◄ In a 1963 story on the trouble-plagued shooting of Cleopatra, this picture of Liz and Richard Burton was headlined LONGEST FILM FINALLY ENDS IN SPAIN . . . BUT ITS CO-STARS JUST DON'T STOP. They were already doing a second movie together, The V.I.P.'s, and soon after, Liz married Burton, her fifth husband.

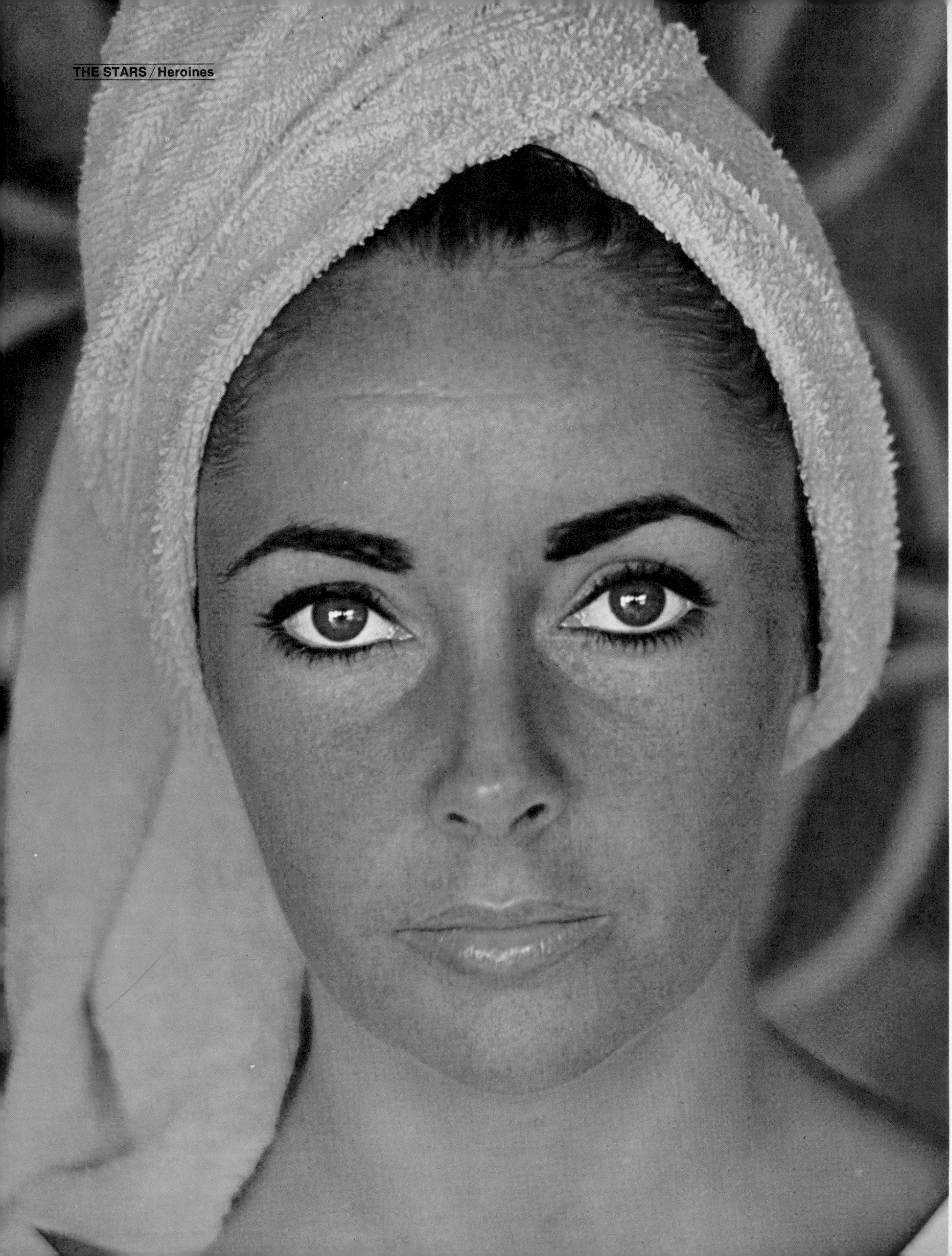

In her first Shakespearean role, as Kate in *The Taming of the Shrew* (1967), Liz flailed at her pursuing suitor Petruchio before fleeing across a rooftop. Petruchio was played by Richard Burton, who confidently told LIFE: "Elizabeth tries to be a shrew . . . (but) is inevitably tamed after a bit of talking."

In a picture accompanying a 1964 cover story in which she was interviewed about her life and marriages, Liz, having her hair done, mugged for the photographer, actor Roddy McDowall, her childhood buddy.

As Martha, the bitchy wife in Edward Albee's *Who's Afraid of Virginia Woolf?* (1966), Liz cringed as she heard her husband George reveal that the child she talked of was a myth. Liz won one of her two Oscars in this role. The other was for *Butterfield 8.*

For the 1964 story, McDowall, who has remained one of Elizabeth's closest friends, "caught her without make-up," LIFE said with a straight face.

More Movie Royalty

Fans flocked to movies that bannered many a female member of Hollywood's nobility. Some quickly faded or disappeared; others reigned long and agelessly.

Gloria Swanson posed before Sunset Boulevard was released in 1950. For the role, make-up men added wrinkles to make her look old enough.

Careers ran long during the '30s and '40s: the studios had too much invested in their top charges to discard them out of hand. Nonetheless, many of the brightest new luminaries dimmed before their time, snuffed out by retirement, untimely death or by the system's prejudice against aging. Photographer Philippe Halsman protested: "Women must be young, whereas a man may still be considered attractive at 50. So young girls must constantly be discovered." His own picture of Gloria Swanson at 51, below, taken in 1950, added considerable weight to his indictment.

Rich girl turned model turned movie queen turned real royalty, picture-book-pretty Grace Kelly wed Prince Rainier of Monaco in 1956 and retired.

Greatly admired for her fine comedic touch, Carole Lombard married Clark Gable in 1939, but tragically lost her life in a 1942 plane crash.

Her chin-up screen suffering in Mrs. Miniver won a 1942 Oscar for Greer Garson, brave green-eyed beauty of '40s flicks. Her career slumped after 1949, but she returned in even nobler roles in the '60s.

The Girl Next Door

Fresh-faced, virginal and uncomplicated, they all seemed to be not inaccessible movie goddesses but outdoorsy and uneccentric versions of anybody's popular kid sister.

Dumped into a basket of tomatoes, wide-eyed Doris Day was once again sitting pretty in The Thrill of It All (1963). That year she was the movie industry's top box-office star—as she was in 1960, 1962 and 1964.

Ginger Rogers was on the cover four times, including this 1942 shot taken while fishing on her Oregon ranch. "She is just beautiful enough," LIFE wrote, "not to be an affront to other women. She believes in God and love and a hard day's work." Like Doris Day, Ginger had an ice-cream soda fountain in her home.

Tiny June Allyson (5 ft. 1 in., 99 lbs. in this 1945 cover picture) was a self-taught dancer who saw one Fred Astaire-Ginger Rogers film 18 times, LIFE said. Always demurely dressed, she made a score of light comedies, went on to soberer, if still syrupy, roles.

The apotheosis of purity, Donna Reed plunked down in a field of wild wheat for this 1946 cover. Cast against type, she earned an Oscar playing the role of a whore in From Here to Eternity (1953).

35

The New Breed

As the traditional big studios went into decline, a different kind of actress emerged. Her art reflected the impact of both the sexual revolution and the brazen counterculture.

Cover girls of a recent era—Barbra Streisand, Julie Christie, Mia Farrow, Candice Bergen and Diana Ross—suggest the change that came to entertainment in the 1960s.

Model Ali MacGraw, a hit in Goodbye, Columbus (1969), had a crooked front tooth she refused to fix for films. She attributed her confidence in part to a happy, pastoral childhood: "I lived in the country and we were a close family who liked each other a lot."

The 1968 cover story on Jane Fonda was inspired by her appearance—largely undressed—in hubby Roger Vadim's Barbarella. LIFE said people had expected Henry Fonda's daughter to behave like the girl next door, and added: "Some girl next door!"

When she made Georgy Girl (1966), Lynn Redgrave —"nearly six feet tall, bluntly outspoken and something of a kook"—was, LIFE noted, "the most toasted actor in Britain's reigning theatrical family." Lynn said she didn't mind "being so damn big."

Wreathed in a free-form tiara that enhanced her flawless face, Catherine Deneuve posed for LIFE in 1969, the year after Belle de Jour was released.

The Heroes

Throughout the years, it was a simple fact of life—if not of LIFE—that the annual Hollywood roster of the Top Ten box-office personalities was predominantly masculine.

In this era of consciousness-raising for women, there is the recurring complaint that screenwriters simply aren't coming up with rewarding roles for actresses—suggesting somehow that things used to be different in the golden good old days. The truth is, Shirley Temple aside, only one female—Betty Grable in the pin-up year of 1943—was ever Number One until the 1960s, when Doris Day reached that pinnacle of popularity four times. Nonetheless, LIFE, ever interested in feminine pulchritude, generally favored the distaff side of the Screen Actors Guild.

Clark Gable had it made both ways. The quintessential Movie Star, Male, he was the King—perennially among the top attractions, as popular with men as with women. But he also appeared often in the magazine's pages because he played opposite every glamorous female M-G-M owned or could latch onto.

As a farm boy, Billy Gable had the biggest feet in Hopedale, Ohio, and jug ears that were affectionately scoffed at long after he had dropped the Billy for Clark, his middle name. But he had a magnetic attraction for women —and vice versa. Having tried many jobs, including stage acting and lumberjacking, he went to Hollywood in 1924 and did only extra work. After a Broadway stint, he got a role in Pathé's *The Painted Desert* in 1930. Then 11 parts came along in 1931 after M-G-M signed him. In one, *A Free Soul,* he slapped Norma Shearer and overnight became famous. By 1932 he was in the Top Ten, and he stayed there until 1943, when he was in the Army Air Force. He was Number Two—to Shirley Temple—three years in a row (1936-1938) and returned to the list in the years 1947–1949.

While Gable always pretended he didn't know much about acting, Spencer Tracy —who also landed his first film contract in 1930 and went on to become the industry's most honored actor—couldn't get away with such self-deprecation. He tried, though, with his much-quoted dictum about a star: "Just know your lines and don't bump into the furniture." So well did he succeed that he won nine Oscar nominations and two awards, the men's record: one more of each than runner-up Laurence Olivier.

Another first-magnitude star, Gary Cooper, from Helena, Montana, got his film start because, while in his teens, a doctor had misdiagnosed a hairline hip fracture suffered in a car accident and suggested horseback riding as therapy. Since the pain caused him to anticipate a horse's every move, he became a superb rider and broke into movies in 1925 as a $10-a-day stunt man in Westerns. In a 105-second walk-on as a doomed flight instructor in the 1927 World War I film *Wings (page 157),* Cooper turned during his final exit and tossed his buddies a casual half-salute. The knightly gesture became a conversation piece, and a distinguished spate of motion pictures followed, from 1929's *The Virginian* to *The Naked Edge,* made while Cooper was terminally ill of cancer in 1960.

"There was an intense bond among the biggest stars of the time," Stanley Flink, a LIFE movie reporter of the 1950s, remembered. "When 'the Big C hit Coop,' as John Wayne put it, and everybody knew it, the old guard—guys like Wayne, Bill Holden, Jimmy Stewart, actors, skilled at simulating feelings —showed their affection wordlessly, but with real tears." In a moving moment of Hollywood history, Stewart accepted an honorary Academy Award for the friend he—but not the public—knew was dying. He compromised the well-kept secret of Cooper's condition simply by blowing his lines when his voice broke.

For more than three decades Clark Gable was the essence of everything film makers looked for: a dedicated professional whose appearance and personality on and off screen was attractive to both sexes.

Clark Gable

Playing an infinite variety of roles—in potboilers, light comedy, costume pieces, and serious drama—he was a dominant presence during a long, unchallenged reign.

Holding the script for his role as a cowboy in Arthur Miller's The Misfits opposite Marilyn Monroe, Gable sat for a 1960 dressing-room interview. He died of a heart attack only days after the story appeared.

Honky Tonk (1941) teamed Clark Gable with Lana Turner, "the most electric combination," noted LIFE, "since Charles Boyer and Hedy Lamarr."

In China Seas (1935) Gable was a skipper torn between two loves, played by Jean Harlow, then at her peak, and Rosalind Russell. Harlow won.

With Vivien Leigh as Scarlett O'Hara, Gable made Gone With the Wind in 1939. It piled up a $77 million gross —the box-office record for over 30 years.

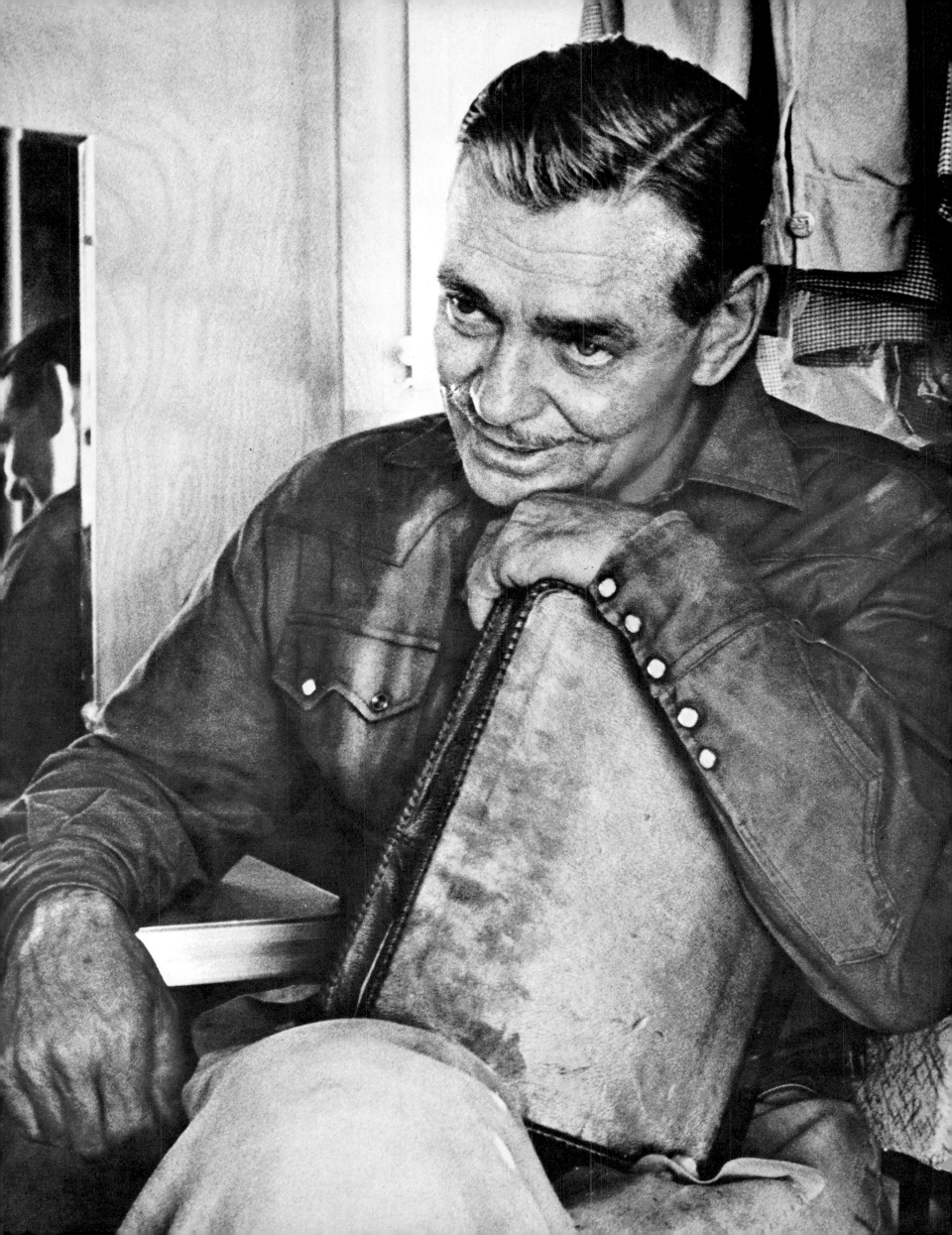

Spencer Tracy

The first major star to appreciate understatement as an important key to the new art of the cinema, he soon won a reputation as the greatest screen actor of his time.

In 1937, having progressed from gangster roles to priests in seven years, Spencer Tracy disguised his red hair and adopted an accent to play a Portuguese fisherman opposite Freddie Bartholomew in Captains Courageous. The result was his first Oscar.

In 1955, as Tracy celebrated his 25th year in movies, a LIFE cover presented his "lumpy but lovable Irish visage." Though he had appeared with nearly every top female star, he himself insisted that he was an "unromantic type" and fought ladies' man roles.

With Myrna Loy in Whipsaw (1935)

With Sylvia Sydney in Fury (1936)

With Joan Crawford in Mannequin (1938)

With Hedy Lamarr in I Take This Woman (1940)

With Claudette Colbert in Boom Town (1940)

Always comfortable to be with, as man or actor, Tracy strides arm-in-arm with Harlow off the set of Riffraff (1936).

43

Gary Cooper

A lanky Montanan with a self-effacing grin drawled his way to particular fame as the archetypal American hero.

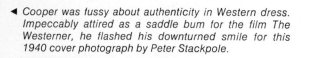
◄ Cooper was fussy about authenticity in Western dress. Impeccably attired as a saddle bum for the film The Westerner, he flashed his downturned smile for this 1940 cover photograph by Peter Stackpole.

Mugging uncharacteristically for a loony LIFE story about fashions in headgear, Coop doffed his ten-gallon hat and tried a guitar-with-chin-strap.

In one of the last photographs ever taken of him, Cooper, knowing that death from cancer was imminent, tenderly touches his inconsolable daughter Maria as his wife "Rocky" smiles valiantly at his side. The picture, "a study in grief, love and courage," accompanied the star's obituary, published in May 1961.

In the chips in 1933, Cooper "splurged on a green-and-yellow Duesenberg." LIFE observed that he loved tinkering with cars and often washed his current favorite himself.

John Wayne

Big and craggy, he carved a sizable niche for himself as the Mr. Clean of countless Westerns. But he won his Oscar as a boozing, aging lawman in 1969's True Grit.

A loving Big John and his son John Ethan, 2, were snapped off-guard on the set of The Sons of Katie Elder. The 1965 film, which Wayne proudly described to LIFE as a real "ridin', jumpin', fightin'" Western, went into production only two months after a malignancy was removed from his chest.

Paunch cinched in, and armed to the teeth, a still formidable Wayne struck this heroic pose for a 1972 story about his role in The Cowboys. In a rare turn for a Western superstar, the Duke played an old cattleman who is shot dead midway in the last reel.

In director John Ford's galloping spectacular of the Civil War, The Horse Soldiers (1959), Unionman Wayne blasted the Confederates. The photographer, Murray Laden, got the shot (both ways).

In The Undefeated (1969), Wayne urged on his wards: 3,000 horses, originally meant for the Mexican government, that he later delivered instead to rebel forces. "Big John," LIFE said of the politically conservative Wayne, "winds up on the side of the revolutionaries, which must have been a nasty shock to him."

47

Bing Crosby

The most relaxed entertainer of them all, the crooner worked hard to make it all look easy. Crises in his private life helped convert him into a fine dramatic actor.

"Serious funny business," LIFE called this shot of a trouserless Bing Crosby rehearsing a ballet to attract Dorothy Lamour in The Road to Bali (1952).

His first wife dead, his second family not yet in sight, Crosby in 1954 was tired, depressed and unsure of his acting ability when he played a drunken, has-been musical comedy star opposite Grace Kelly in The Country Girl. Probably his finest performance, it started one of show business's classic comebacks.

Barry Fitzgerald and Crosby watch their church burn in Going My Way (1944). Bing won his only Oscar portraying the fun-loving priest in this film—indeed an acting tour de force in view of the personal turmoil already besetting him. But LIFE suggested that his work in The Country Girl was more deserving.

Rehearsing for a 1962 TV special, Crosby joyfully collapses with Bob Hope, friend and professional sidekick through many a TV and radio skit, and all those Road pictures.

Frank Sinatra

Ol' Blue Eyes not only succeeded Bing Crosby as The Supersinger, but like him won a new lease on his professional life with a great dramatic performance.

His career at rock bottom, Sinatra bounced right back in From Here to Eternity (1953) as a bullied GI who dies in Montgomery Clift's arms.

When LIFE ran this photograph of Sinatra singing "As Time Goes By" in New York's Riobamba in 1943, the skinny 25-year-old alumnus of the Harry James and Tommy Dorsey bands was making $250,000 a year performing in clubs, theaters and films.

Sinatra was considerably heavier, in every sense of the word, when John Dominis photographed him for a 1965 cover story. LIFE's article, detailing Sinatra acts of public arrogance and private kindness, ventured to say that the singer was "the most controversial, powerful and surprising entertainer around."

Sinatra had covers at 50 and on his retirement (kind of) at 55.

Marlon Brando

Transplanted to Hollywood from the Broadway stage, his potent and many-sided talent exploded on the screen and presaged a revolutionary new style in movie acting.

In Viva Zapata! (1952), Marlon Brando essayed a brooding and passionate interpretation of the life of Emiliano Zapata, the Mexican guerrilla.

Seeking the right speech lilt, Brando ate in a Japanese restaurant and spoke Japanese to the waiters while preparing for his rare comedic role in Teahouse of the August Moon (1956). Not necessary, said LIFE flippantly, noting that "his celebrated mumble could be an approximation of Okinawan speech."

As Stanley Kowalski in Tennessee Williams' highly ac- ▶ claimed A Streetcar Named Desire (1951), Brando launched a startlingly different kind of film character: a brawling, blatantly virile animal who seemed to leap out of the screen at the audience.

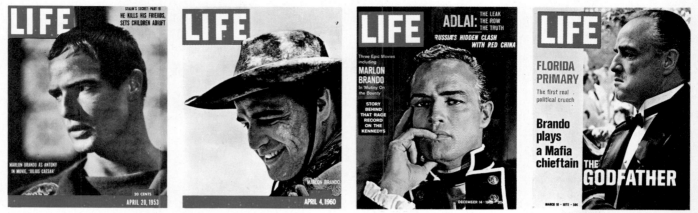

Four LIFE covers—the record for male stars—charted Brando's rise, from Mark Antony in *Julius Caesar* to *The Godfather*'s ruthless Don.

Don Vito Corleone, the aging Mafioso in The Godfather ▶ (1972), soaked up sun in the garden of his suburban compound. The gangster epic surpassed Gone With the Wind as the greatest box-office attraction of all time, and it earned Brando his second Oscar—which the maverick actor refused to accept.

In On the Waterfront, a stoic Brando was comforted by Eva Marie Saint after a beating by organized thugs. His portrayal of a hard-headed, working-class loner won the young star 1954's Oscar as Best Actor.

The young star from Streetcar turned up playing the recorder in a 1948 story on ''The Brandos'' that also dealt with his talented sister, actress Jocelyn.

''These are hard things to get right,'' Brando soothingly told Pina Pellicer while directing, starring in and spending double the budget of the Western One-Eyed Jacks (1961).

The Matinee Idols

The movie public always backed its favorites, so many of these tall, dark (or blond) and handsome leading men played the same role over and over again: themselves.

Gregory Peck, costumed for Twelve O'Clock High (1950), lifts his eyebrows in a trademark arch. LIFE had predicted five years earlier that his Lincolnesque face would make feminine fans ecstatic. It did.

There were many male performers who, besides acting skill (or sometimes in place of it), had the audience-pleasing ability to play themselves over and over even as they were cast in a variety of roles—and thus contributed mightily to the greening of Hollywood.

Inevitably, they fell into categories. The matinee idols, like such silent-screen forebears as Wallace Reid and Conrad Nagel, could play any character as long as he was the right age (young) and was a Hero. The tough guys were more limited; they did not have to play heavies (villains)—although they could and sometimes did—but they were expected to act masculine to the point of either belting somebody or theatening to. The character actors had a problem: *their* virtuosity threatened to typecast them forever in those great minor roles that made movies work.

Professionals who did not blanch at the challenge of Shakespeare were respectfully referred to by some as Actors, in contradistinction to the likes of Gable, who told LIFE's James Goode shortly before he died: "I don't know what they mean by 'finished actor.' As far as I know, finished is when you can't get a job." Such categorization went by the board when the New Breed took hold in the 1960s.

Visiting William Randolph Hearst's ornate estate in ▶ 1938, gangling Jimmy Stewart—he of the aw-shucks drawl—still managed to look underwhelmed.

The name was Roy Fitzgerald, and nothing happened. The name Rock Hudson was attached to the same face and six-foot-three frame, and suddenly he became a box-office bonanza. This shot was a 1955 cover, after Magnificent Obsession grossed $8 million.

Tasmanian-born adventurer Errol Flynn, LIFE said in 1938, irked his bosses by "periodically running away to sail his boat or get into a war."

Fans deluged perpetually boyish Van Johnson with boxes of candy and cookies, and made him, LIFE said in 1945, "the most adored male in the U.S."

The Tough Guys

They snarled, sneered or strode panther-like through scores of movies exuding menace and machismo—and by their work added a new dimension to films: reality.

Cigarette tilted at a defiant angle, Jean-Paul Belmondo starred in the cops-and-robbers French film *Breathless* (1961), a pell-mell drama that left audiences in similar condition. LIFE lauded the Gallic Bogart as "an engaging, cock-of-the-walk punklet."

The tattoo on Robert Mitchum's right hand spelled LOVE, but the HATE on his left was more to the point of *The Night of the Hunter* (1955), an offbeat chiller about a bogus preacher intent on killing two children in order to steal money left them by their father.

Irish-Mexican Anthony Quinn, interviewed in 1963, re-affirmed his determination not to be typecast. Quinn crashed Hollywood as a fake Indian in 1936, played dozens of nationalities, and eventually won two Oscars —as a Mexican bandit in Viva Zapata! (1952) and as the artist Gauguin in Lust for Life (1956).

Burt Lancaster's coiled intensity was first projected in The Killers (1946). Once an acrobat, he foreshadowed the New Breed of film actor and went on to become one of the early independent actor-producers.

Humphrey Bogart got an Oscar for his boozy captain in The African Queen (1951) and became a posthumous cult hero. The prototypal tough guy, he was a top box-office draw for years, despite a slight impediment of speech and a face, LIFE observed that "looks as if it had just smelled something unpleasant."

The Characters

*Was that Guinness in drag? Ustinov under the shako?
A cap or boater became the key to the character, and
make-up and costuming added immeasurably to the fun.*

*In Romanoff and Juliet (1961), a mincing Peter Ustinov ▶
showed why LIFE felt he was versatile enough to mimic
"motors, Ping-Pong balls and diplomats."*

*During the '60s, when honest faces were finally "in,"
Walter Matthau leaped from quirky minor roles to quirky
leads, as in The Odd Couple (1968).*

When it came to disguises and mimicry, perhaps no one since the heyday of Lon Chaney was so clearly the champion as Britain's Sir Alec Guinness.

Guinness looked aloof as Disraeli in The Mudlark (1950) . . .

. . . dapper as Pocket in Great Expectations (1946) . . .

. . . gaunt and bearded as Fagin in Oliver Twist (1948) . . .

. . . prim in his multiroled Kind Hearts and Coronets (1949).

Established as a brilliant, often wildly zany comic actor with a flawless sense of timing, Jack Lemmon—mixing his usual euphoria with the dark despair of a dedicated drunk—gave proof in Days of Wine and Roses (1962) that his art also included great depth.

The New Breed

*In the '60s a cool, confident kind of male animal burst
on the cinema scene: a maverick whose movies reflected
an undercurrent of rebellion that was abroad in the land.*

Of Clint Eastwood, the stony-faced cop in Dirty Harry
(1971), LIFE commented, ''It has been said he learned
to act at the Mt. Rushmore Dramatic Academy.''

*James Dean, here walking through a moody drizzle,
made two 1955 films, East of Eden and Rebel Without a
Cause. Both prefigured the counterculture.*

Steve McQueen drew LIFE's 1963 admiration as ''an
oddball with the cockiness of Cagney, the glower of Bogart, the rough-diamond glow of Garfield.''

Paul Newman and Robert Redford paired for Butch Cassidy and the Sundance Kid (1969). It grossed $44 million and made Redford a big draw.

Although studio bigwigs wanted a leading-man type to be the heir apparent of The Godfather (1972), Al Pacino got the job on sheer acting ability.

Warren Beatty, LIFE said in 1961, would turn the ''charms of James Dean and looks of Brando'' into gold. He did, in Bonnie and Clyde (1967).

63

The Sex Symbols

*Before Marilyn and after Marilyn—from blonde bombshell
to pin-up, from kitten to censored—LIFE had a thing
about the lasses, both the domestic and imported variety.*

One of LIFE's earliest covers, May 3, 1937, was devoted to a sultry platinum blonde, 26-year-old Jean Harlow, and one of its last featured Raquel Welch as a roller-racing queen. Both were, of course, established names by the time they got such coveted display. But any aspiring actress with some evident promise and a lot of glandular magic had at least a chance, even if the odds were long, at the game of editorial roulette.

Representative was the unknown youngster, Ann-Margret Olson, who started the wheel spinning the moment she walked into the Los Angeles office one day in 1960. "She was," recalled Dick Stolley, then the bureau chief, "wearing the tightest jersey I'd ever seen. All the typewriters stopped. There was absolute silence, and the temperature went up by 20 degrees." A year later Ann-Margret's new friends covered her screen test for a musical, and—you guessed it—she was on her way to S-T-A-R-D-O-M.

Normally, LIFE's editors went out to discover their own future stars. One day in 1941 correspondent Richard Pollard, on the lookout for a "Picture of the Week," found that a young starlet named Rita Hayworth had the day off. He picked up photographer Bob Landry and went to her house. They found Rita, who had been alerted by her press agent, dressed in a sexy black-and-white nightgown. A bed was selected as an appropriate prop and, while she rearranged herself between takes, Pollard spoke up. "Rita," he said, "take a deep breath." She did, and Landry snapped a photograph *(page 69)* that was to become the most popular girly picture of World War II and probably of all time. Over the years it ran in LIFE nine times.

Marilyn Monroe attracted the editors' attention because of what the magazine described as "a vital, almost atomic capacity to project her sexuality." According to Philippe Halsman, who went to Marilyn's apartment to compose her first cover photograph *(opposite)*, he asked her to stand in the corner of the room. "I was facing her with my camera," he recalls, "and one of the bureau correspondents and my assistant were on each side of me. Such was her talent that each one of us felt, if only the other two would leave, something incredible would happen."

A year later, LIFE photographer Alfred Eisenstaedt, an old-world gentleman noted for bringing out the maternal instincts of his female subjects, went West to take Marilyn's picture. In mid-session, she suddenly sat in his lap, leaned over and kissed him. Eisie, who had photographed emperors and kings, was so flustered he failed to check his camera as he switched between color and black-and-white film. He lost half his shots.

The sex symbols of early days were, in the main, home-grown, but as postwar America matured it looked increasingly to Europeans for sex appeal. An ability to act was no particular deterrent to their popularity, and one of them, Sophia Loren, won an Academy Award—for best actress in her 1961 movie *Two Women*. Sophia was one sex goddess refreshingly unconcerned with her physical attributes: "Beauty is no handicap," she once said "if you don't think about it too much." In 1964, when LIFE did a story on her new villa in Italy, Sophia was dressed in a Dior while Eisenstaedt crawled about entangled in the wires of the lighting equipment. Finally Sophia, who had spent most of her life with lights and cameras, hoisted her skirt, got down on her hands and knees and helped out. Then she rose unruffled. "Okay," she said regally, "just check the light meter and let's shoot."

In 1952 Philippe Halsman posed the emerging starlet Marilyn Monroe in the angle between her clothes closet and the apartment wall. Her shoulders bent forward, she smiled her heavy-lidded smile and the classic picture made her first LIFE cover.

Marilyn Monroe

The story of her life, tragically true, read like one of Hollywood's tear-jerkers: the dreaming foster child who became an international sensation and died at 36.

During a tour of Korea in 1954, Marilyn shoehorned herself into a slinky dress and, shrugging off zero temperatures, launched into a torrid rendition of "Anything Goes" as lonely GIs whistled and howled.

Between 1952 when she was still a starlet, and 1972, 10 years after her death, Marilyn appeared on LIFE's cover nine times—more than anyone except Elizabeth Taylor.

In 1949, hungry and struggling and in need of the modeling fee, Marilyn posed for this nude calendar photograph. LIFE deliberately gave the picture its first circulation nationally, along with a sympathetic account of her difficulties at the time it was taken.

With a 1962 story recapitulating her star-crossed passage, the magazine ran this disarming picture of Marilyn at 19. ''Already,'' said LIFE, she ''had the look of a girl who was made to be remembered.''

The Evolution of "It"

What they had in common was something America had once called "It." No one could say what It was, exactly —but when an actress had it, everybody knew instantly.

Budding starlet Lana Turner promotes her career in 1940 by showing up, dressed to the thirty-nines, at a publicity wing-ding for a swank new hotel.

By the time red-haired Clara Bow played a charmingly naughty flapper in It (1927), she had established the word as the decade's synonym for sex appeal.

After nine years of films, Jean Harlow was The Sex Symbol when this picture appeared on a May 1937 cover. A month later she was dead, at 26.

Mimicking the publicity poses of the '20s, Kim Novak in 1957 makes like the dramatic actress Jeanne Eagels, languishing invitingly on a tiger-skin rug.

Bob Landry's historic 1941 shot of Rita Hayworth benefited from a fluke: a flash bulb that failed to go off improved on the starlet's natural endowments by adding unexpected accenting shadows.

In 1940 Carole Landis' flack labeled her the "Ping Girl." He squeezed mileage out of this picture by having her protest its publication. The press played the story big, calling her a "fugitive from leg art."

69

In 1945 a topless Natalie Wood, at 7 a veteran of three movies, watched her cat lap milk. In 1963 Natalie, obviously grown up, was the subject of a LIFE story: ''Born To Be a Star.'' As the camera clicked, a friend urged her to act ''slightly sensuous''; predictably, she had difficulties with the ''slightly'' part.

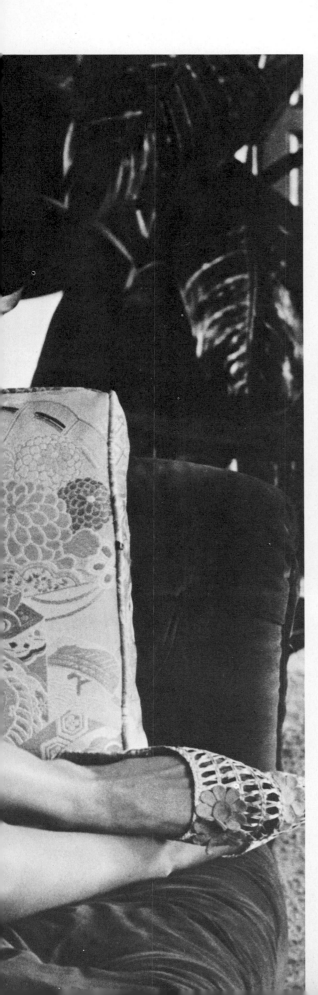

Raquel Welch's starring role as a roller-skate racer in *The Kansas City Bomber* (1972) led to a LIFE appraisal as "the hottest thing on wheels."

While being tested for a new *State Fair* (1962), Ann-Margret Olson (born Olson, but a name-dropper) belted a song aided by her special body English.

Beauties from Europe

Like wines, some foreign imports were heady or sensual, some were saucy or touched with grandeur, and some had sparkle. The best of them traveled very well indeed.

Few noted or long remembered that Gina Lollobrigida was first signed by Howard Hughes. This picture was in a 1951 roundup on Italian actresses.

In her first starring role, Anita Ekberg, from Sweden and blonde as aquavit, played an Indian dancer in (of course you remember it) Zarak (1956).

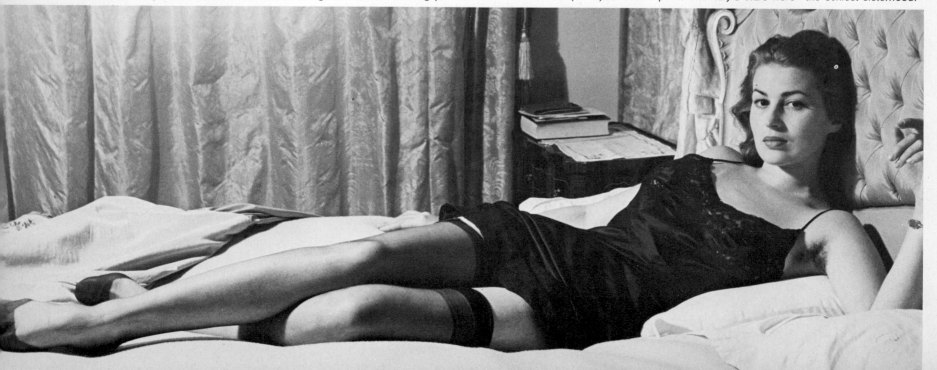

Turned on, the magazine's editor cited Silvana Mangano's blood-warming performance in Bitter Rice (1950) as added proof that Italy's stars were "the sexiest sisterhood."

Peering over Jeanne Moreau's shoulder at her Côte d'Azur villa shortly before her 40th birthday in 1967, LIFE said the day was "just another milestone in her ascendency as a symbol of ageless seduction."

Covering Brigitte Bardot in Spain for the filming of The Lady and the Puppet (1959), a reporter concluded that her "flat and sullen stare" provoked the lust that was the key to her international popularity.

Director Louis Malle brought Moreau and Bardot together for Viva Maria! (1965) and the press flocked to Mexico to see the fireworks. There were none.

. . . And of Course, Sophia

She was a Neapolitan urchin who blossomed (Mamma mia!) into an earth mother with style and wit. Chaplin noted the rare blend of regal bearing and clown's heart.

Sophia was featured seven times on covers: playing a fishmonger, as

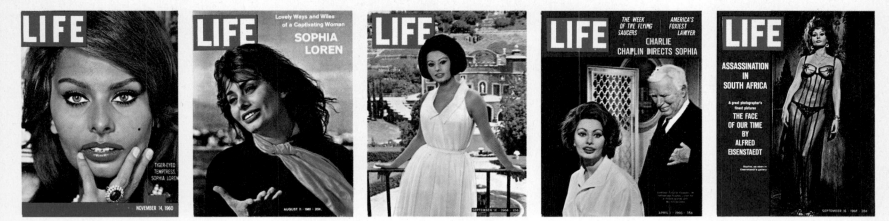

wcomer to the film capital, sensuous, candid, at her splendid new Roman villa, making a movie under Charlie Chaplin's direction, and in something like a negligee.

Loren playfully planted a kick on a pal's posterior while Alfred Eisenstaedt was photographing a 1961 story titled "Part Goddess, Part Imp, All Woman."

Sophia joked about her famous figure to friend and confidante Dora Jane Hamblin of LIFE. "Everything you see," she said, "I owe to spaghetti."

75

The Clowns

In the earliest days of the motion pictures, comedy was king. Out of it came the industry's most unforgettable —and stormy—character and its one undisputed genius.

In the beginning, the most famous actors were clowns. The greatest was Charlie Chaplin. (It paid well, too. As early as 1916 he received a $670,000 bonus, in addition to his $10,000-a-week salary, for 12 two-reelers.) Half of a stormy lifetime before his achievements won a knighthood, Chaplin was an acknowledged film genius. George Bernard Shaw said so (he called him the *only* one), and so did James Agee, the poet-critic who in 1949 wrote LIFE's definitive article on screen comedy, "Comedy's Greatest Era." But to Agee—and to the millions who had roared at the pratfalls and pants-afire sprints of Mack Sennett's zanies of the 1910s and '20s, other clowns, with other styles, *could* hold a candle to him. Agee did approvingly quote Sennett's assertion that Chaplin was "just the greatest artist that ever lived," but he also loved stone-faced Buster Keaton, cross-eyed Ben Turpin, and Harold Lloyd and Harry Langdon.

London-born Chaplin, the product of poverty and English music halls, became the complete and unrivaled master of the motion-picture medium—a creative one-man band. He proved it in 1952 when he delivered a masterpiece—a musical masterpiece, no less—in *Limelight* and did it as nearly single-handedly as is possible in such a complicated art. He conceived the film, wrote the screenplay, directed it, played the lead, composed and conducted the score, designed the costumes and choreographed the dance numbers.

But the baggy-trousered, indomitable foil of fate whom Chaplin invented while working for Mack Sennett in 1914 had marked his creator for all time as *sui generis*. The Tramp was, said Agee, "as centrally representative of humanity, as many-sided and mysterious, as Hamlet . . . it seems unlikely that any dancer or actor can have excelled him in eloquence,

variety or poignancy of motion." The Tramp's wistful, fragile figure brought pathos and hilarity together. "He was the first man," Agee concluded, who was able "to give the silent language a soul."

When *City Lights* (1931) was reissued in 1950, the magazine's editors reminded its younger readers that the film was based on the classic tragicomic Charlie Chaplin story: "the tender-hearted tramp moving with imperturbable finesse through one terrifying complexity after another," including a love affair with a blind girl to whom he pretended to be handsome and rich. Of the same movie, Agee had said its final scene, in which the cured girl sees her friend for the first time, was "the highest moment in movies."

Chaplin's perfectionism was legendary. So was that of W. Eugene Smith, the LIFE photographer who pioneered the photographic essay. The editors worked hard to get Chaplin's permission to open the set so that Smith might cover the making of *Limelight,* and the result was a classic confrontation of men with similar standards. Smith, with reporter Stanley Flink in tow, was on the set every day, and Chaplin developed a deep respect for the photographer's total immersion in his work. At last, Chaplin's assistant director, Robert Aldrich (who was himself to become one of the industry's toughest and most successful directors), took Flink aside and told him privately that the LIFE team "has cost us about $300,000 so far." When Flink asked what he was talking about, Aldrich explained that Chaplin was determined to keep reshooting each scene until he got a take that made Smith smile. Because "that goddam photographer" was so serious, Aldrich said, Chaplin, who normally averaged two or three takes per scene, was shooting as many as 15.

Just before leaving the U.S. in 1952 for his self-imposed Swiss exile, Chaplin volunteered this pose for famed photographer Richard Avedon.

Charlie Chaplin

His production of Limelight may stand forever as an unparalleled example of movie-making virtuosity. He wore all the creative hats—except the Tramp's trademark derby.

Critic James Agee called the scene from which this still was taken "the highest moment in movies." It is the end of City Lights (1931); the Tramp has just confessed to the girl who has regained her sight that he is her supposedly rich, handsome benefactor.

In a pause while filming Limelight in 1952, Chaplin hugs daughter Josephine, 3, before sending her off to play. She and two siblings of his marriage to Oona O'Neill appeared in a scene. For all the controversy about Chaplin's private life, in this period he was, according to LIFE, "a fond father."

◄ After rehearsing the orchestra and setting up other actors for the camera, Chaplin steps in front of the lens to do a music-hall number he wrote.

As the Limelight staff watches, Chaplin rehearses dancers for the ballet he choreographed. Buster Keaton, in waiter's vest, stands by for his own comic bit.

The Great Comic Tradition

Chaplin and his great silent-screen contemporaries left a heritage that has entertained movie-goers ever since, through a lengthy roster of gifted (and vocal) emulators.

Sound altered screen comedy and ended the careers of some masters of a highly demanding art. To command the rich vocabulary of visual clichés—the pratfalls, the double and triple takes, the teetering on precarious perches—a performer had to combine the skills of acrobat, dancer, clown and mime.

Ben Turpin had all these skills, but he did not adapt his broad style to the talkies, whose tight sets and immobile cameras—required because the early microphones lacked discrimination—took the laughs out of his low comedy. He was lost.

In Love Happy (1949), his last film, Harpo, whom LIFE called the "silent frenzy of the Marx Brothers," registered triumph by jetting smoke from his ears.

Flirting with disaster in Hard Luck (1921), balletically gifted Buster Keaton put a world of character into a simple exercise in balance.

Buster Keaton, also a master of mime, tried the transition, but did so by signing with a big studio. There he found no room for the improvisation basic to his art and was soon reduced to small parts.

Happily, the comic vocabulary of these stars did not die with them; it passed on to their artistic heirs. At least one Marx Brother retained the prerogatives of silent comedy by simply refusing to speak. And, although the latter-day zanies such as Jerry Lewis, Jackie Gleason, Lucille Ball and Bob Hope talked a blue streak, they also echoed the screen techniques of the early movie clowns.

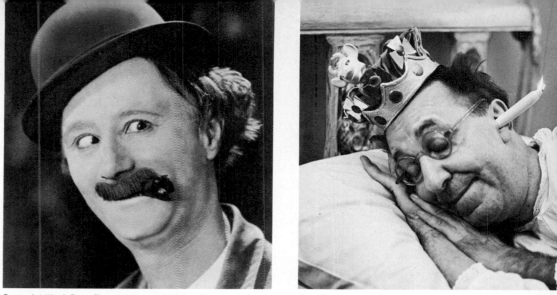

Sound killed Ben Turpin's career; Ed Wynn's thrived on wild sight gags, like this alarm-clock candle. in 1944.

When LIFE ran this cover shot of Dean Martin and Jerry Lewis in 1951, the rakish singer and the master mugger were the top money act in show business. They separated in 1956—Dino to become a prime movie and TV star; Jerry as a star director and—Surprise!—cult figure to French cinema buffs.

Jackie Gleason won fame delivering funny lines on TV, but in 1962 he echoed Chaplin by writing and starring in Gigot. As an affecting mute who finds joy in just being alive, he amuses neighborhood kids simply by kiting a leaf with his own breath.

Long before Lucille Ball developed on TV into that rarest of talents, the female clown, she had honed her comic skills in movies, of which she made more than 50. This picture accompanied a 1962 LIFE story celebrating her return to TV in a new series.

Strung on invisible wires, Bob Hope zipped across the landscape in The Paleface (1948). Hailed as the greatest stand-up comic of all time, in his movie work he leaned heavily on weird costumes and visual gags.

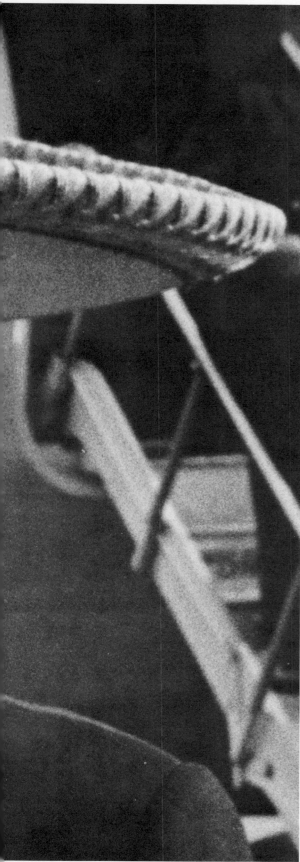

For a 1962 cover story on the "Hilarious Heyday of Eternal Hope," Bob donned an oversized sombrero. The master of the speedy quip was quietly parlaying his popularity into a great personal fortune.

With Bing Crosby, a perennial pal both on and off the screen, Hope strutted in Road to Utopia (1946). It was the fourth of seven gold-paved Road films they made together, usually with side-kick Dorothy Lamour.

In a unique and productive parlay of Hollywood press agentry and LIFE's prestige, hundreds of lovely nonentities became famous overnight—many of them for little longer than that. Those few with the talent and fortitude to match their pulchritude actually made it into the movies. The rest of them vanished without a trace.

The Buildup

In the Hollywood of the '30s and '40s, stars were not born; they were mass produced. The machinery that swallowed up legions of girls with pretty midwestern faces and that ground out sultry vamps and sexy hoydens gave each young hopeful a buildup that can only be described as relentless.

Not every starlet survived this process. A girl had to have stamina to match her beauty in order to reach the top and stay there—or, for that matter, merely to endure the buildup. There may have been some differences between Debbie Reynolds' fresh-faced effervescence and Rita Hayworth's steamy sex appeal, or Lana Turner's earthy grace and Jeanne Crain's bubbly ingenuousness, but what they all shared was a driving determination that gave them an advantage over the hundreds of pretty and equally publicized (though often less gifted) rivals.

The full-dress Hollywood buildup usually amounted to a complete metamorphosis. The budding neophyte was subjected to make-up classes and voice classes; she took deportment lessons, posture lessons and lessons in how to dress. But even more important than her transformation was her publicity. Studio press representatives had her squired to the right spots with the right dates and tried to wangle mentions of her in the columns of Hedda Hopper, Louella Parsons and Sidney Skolsky. She was photographed in every imaginable pose, and a few unimaginable ones, and the results were sent to almost any publication with a circulation of over 10.

With such a heavy-duty promotion machine in operation, Hollywood's press agents were quick to recognize a godsend when they saw one: the new, prestigious national picture magazine that appeared in 1936. A *picture* magazine. To them it seemed a publication tailor-made for their great buildup. So it was only natural that from late 1936 through World War II and into the later '40s, LIFE was inundated with such a flood of publicity pictures that its Los Angeles bureau (which was actually in Beverly Hills) became second only to Washington as a story source for the editors in New York.

Recognizing their own godsend when they saw it, the magazine adopted a pragmatic editorial stance that served it well for more than two decades. The humorist's adjective for this attitude would be "deadpan." With a perfectly straight face, only barely disguising the tongue in the cheek, LIFE published the most egregious specimens of studio publicity, innocently imparting to them all the sparkling photographic appeal that the magazine's large size, its glossy paper and its highly touted presswork added. The most notorious example of LIFE's mock-serious style was headlined "Released for Publication"

(page 88). Thus LIFE's readers discovered that they could have their cheesecake and enjoy it too.

In this somewhat uneasy but mutually advantageous alliance, LIFE even improved, if that is the word, on the studios' inventiveness in pushing their protégés. Recognizing the obvious advantage of the pretty-girl picture in adding froth to issues heavy with politics and war, LIFE's editors and photographers proved to be every bit as ingenious and imaginative as the Hollywood flacks, and at times even more implausible. Probably the best practitioner of this art was Peter Stackpole, one of the magazine's first four staff photographers (the others: Margaret Bourke-White, Alfred Eisenstaedt and Tom McAvoy). With the willing assistance of the press agents, Stackpole would collect a group of girls and produce situations often as long on absurdity as they were short on clothing. One such was a 1945 game of strip poker involving, among others, actresses Ann Miller and Nina Foch. Taken to a chilly Hollywood backyard, the girls shivered and partially stripped —all for the benefit not only of LIFE, but of World War II refugees: the clothes they lost were "donated to war relief."

Another LIFE photographer with a flair for such invention was John Florea. One of his most useful contributions to home-front morale was a photograph of popular pin-up Jane Russell standing modestly on the torpedo-damaged hull of a warship, a finger to her lips as she displayed a sign that read, "A SLIP OF THE LIP WILL SINK A SHIP." Like many other LIFE photographers, Florea found himself frantically shuttling between World War II battle theaters and Hollywood sets. Florea, now a film producer-director, recalls that "In the middle of a Hollywood job they'd say, 'Hey, you're needed in the South Pacific,' and off I'd go. It seemed a little unreal."

The combined talents of LIFE and Hollywood were in large part responsible for that phenomenon of World War II, the pin-up picture. But by the end of the war there was a decline in demand, coinciding with the waning of the Star System. Hollywood's machinery for discovering, grooming and touting the star-to-be went into eclipse. At the same time, possibly for similar reasons, the editors found that the pretty-girl cover was beginning to lose its traditional attraction on the newsstands. By the mid-1960s a pretty face on the cover was just not enough. A unique marriage of ingénue and ingenuity thereby came to a gradual end—along with a lot of foolishness and a lot of fun.

Debbie Reynolds, Lana Turner, Rita Hayworth, Jeanne Crain—all four made it as cover girls when they were on the brink of making it big in films.

LIFE

DEBBIE REYNOLDS
THE STORY BEHIND A COVER

20 CENTS

FEBRUARY 26, 1951
CIRCULATION OVER
5,200,000

LIFE

STARLET LANA TURNER

JANUARY 29, 1940 **10** CENTS

LIFE

RITA HAYWORTH

AUGUST 11, 1941 **10** CENTS
YEARLY SUBSCRIPTION $4.50

LIFE

JEANNE CRAIN
IN BUBBLE BATH

SEPTEMBER 30, 1946 **15** CENTS
YEARLY SUBSCRIPTION $5.50

"Released for Publication"

Using this mock-serious title, LIFE's editors in the late '30s adorned their pages with Hollywood's wondrous press agentry and commented on it in deadpan captions.

In a California army unit in 1942, a faithful fan, Private Albert Goetz, inspired by Jane Russell's pin-up, knits a sweater for her. He had trouble finishing the job: his buddies stole his needles. Miss Russell's agent saw fit to record Goetz's act of devotion and submitted the picture for publication in LIFE.

Merrilyn Grix and Kathy Marlowe (reading from upper to lower) smile bravely as they turn on a kind of rotis-serie spit in a 1956 demonstration purporting to show the power of the small electric motor near their heads. LIFE also noted that Kathy had previously been elected "Miss Dents Out of Fenders."

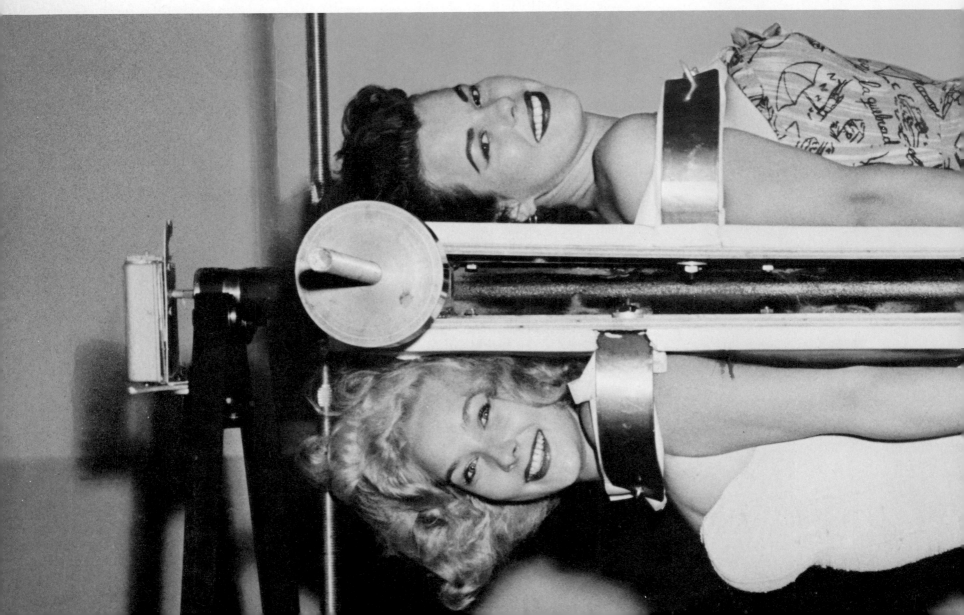

◄ The fertile imagination of photographer John Florea put starlet Eleanor Counts under a vat of California champagne in 1941, letting the drips fall where they might. In an astonishing display of misjudgment, LIFE's editors first rejected the picture as too corny; they later bought it from the Associated Press.

"The silliest publicity picture to come out of Hollywood ► this spring," said LIFE in what may have been the understatement of 1947. The leggy lovely shaking hands with the hanger-on is Arlene Dahl, just voted Miss Edelbrew of 1946; the boy is Philip Wilk, winner of first prize in a high-school chinning meet.

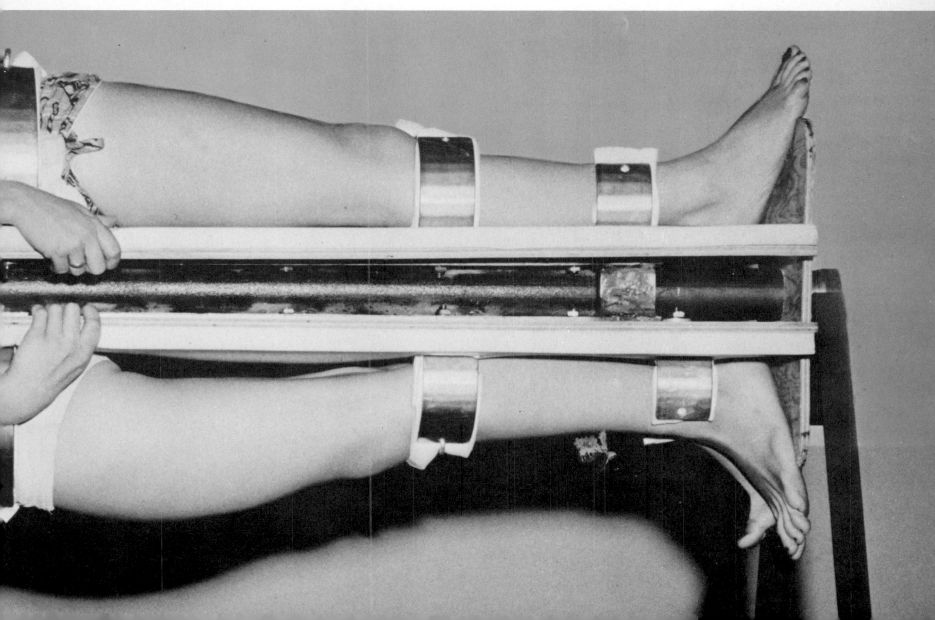

A lot of screen beauties bathed for the camera, catching the public eye by getting suds in i

Marlene Dietrich, 1937

Ava Gardner, 1948

Paulette Goddard, 1949

Myrna Loy, 1933

Jane Russell, 1954

Olivia de Havilland, 1943

Marilyn Monroe and Victor Moore, 1955

June Preisser, 1940

Everybody who was anybody readily came clean for the photographer – even Little Caesar.

Lorraine Gettman and Myrna Dell, 1941

Lana Turner, 1941

Sandra Giles, 1958

Ann Sheridan, 1956

Joanne Woodward, 1958

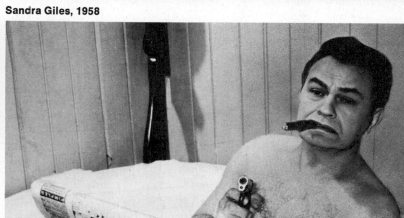

Edward G. Robinson, 1948

"A Good Girl Act By Wednesday"

To balance the war news, LIFE photographers responded with inspiration and desperation to steady requests from the New York editors for pictures of starlets at play.

Not content with what Hollywood's press agents were already providing for them, and anxious to offset all the pictures of bad news, LIFE's New York editors would regularly cable the Los Angeles bureau: "Need good girl act by Wednesday for issue balance." The West Coast always came through. In their inspiration—and desperation—and often hanging their rationale on invisible news pegs, photographers Peter Stackpole, John Florea, Bob Landry and their colleagues cooked up zanier situations than anything conceived by the most fevered Hollywood studio flacks.

In an unlikely version of the Starlet-Wakes-Up cliché, Peter Stackpole took pictures of aspiring Barbara Hale at an Arizona dude ranch in 1946, climbing out of her bedroll and primping in her long johns.

◄ *Poetically named Sunnie O'Dea gives Stackpole a demonstration of her pirouette style in 1941, coincidentally providing LIFE with a kaleidoscope of twirling legs, flying petticoats and lacy underwear.*

"Hollywood's newest way of throwing a party," LIFE called this in 1940. Stackpole assembled Ann Rutherford (center) and friends Arleen Whelan and Alexander D'Arcy, who improvised with a hose.

Jean Colleran, Peggy Lloyd and Betty Jane Hess interpret the classic Three Graces pose for John Florea in 1943. The girls were models brought to Hollywood for Columbia's movie Cover Girl.

Esther Williams, a swimming champion and contender for the Most Waterlogged Actress award, submerges as a netted mermaid in a Los Angeles swimming pool for LIFE's Eliot Elisofon in 1946.

Shapely Sheree North heads south over a hurdle to show that she is on the right track to replace Marilyn Monroe. Loomis Dean's 1955 picture indicated that Sheree could fill the role.

Carole Ohmart does a creditable imitation of an Egyptian bust for LIFE's Don Ornitz. When Ornitz found she was one-sixteenth Egyptian, he buried about eleven sixteenths of her in Malibu Beach sand. ▶

To announce her part in Ziegfeld Follies in 1944, model Eve Whitney assumes—complete with a cordless phone—a pose familiar to the fans of pin-up artist George Petty.

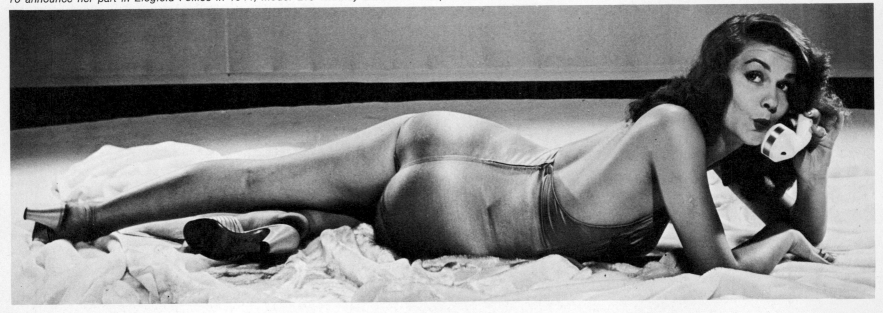

Virginia Gilmore (ascending) was named owner of Hollywood's prettiest legs in a 1939 contest. Virginia Counts protested that her legs were just as pretty. Peter Stackpole happened to be there when the two met picturesquely to contest the title.

Helen Perry, her press agent claimed, preferred to wear her nightie when she played her bass fiddle. LIFE reported that Helen was not only a musician but a mother, a model and—by the way—a bit player in the 1948 movie, The Velvet Touch.

Dona Drake was not a musician, but she found it helpful to dress, her agent told photographer Stackpole, in what she called her violin suit. Thus attired, she could better wield the bow for her role in a film that never hit the screen, Murder Farm.

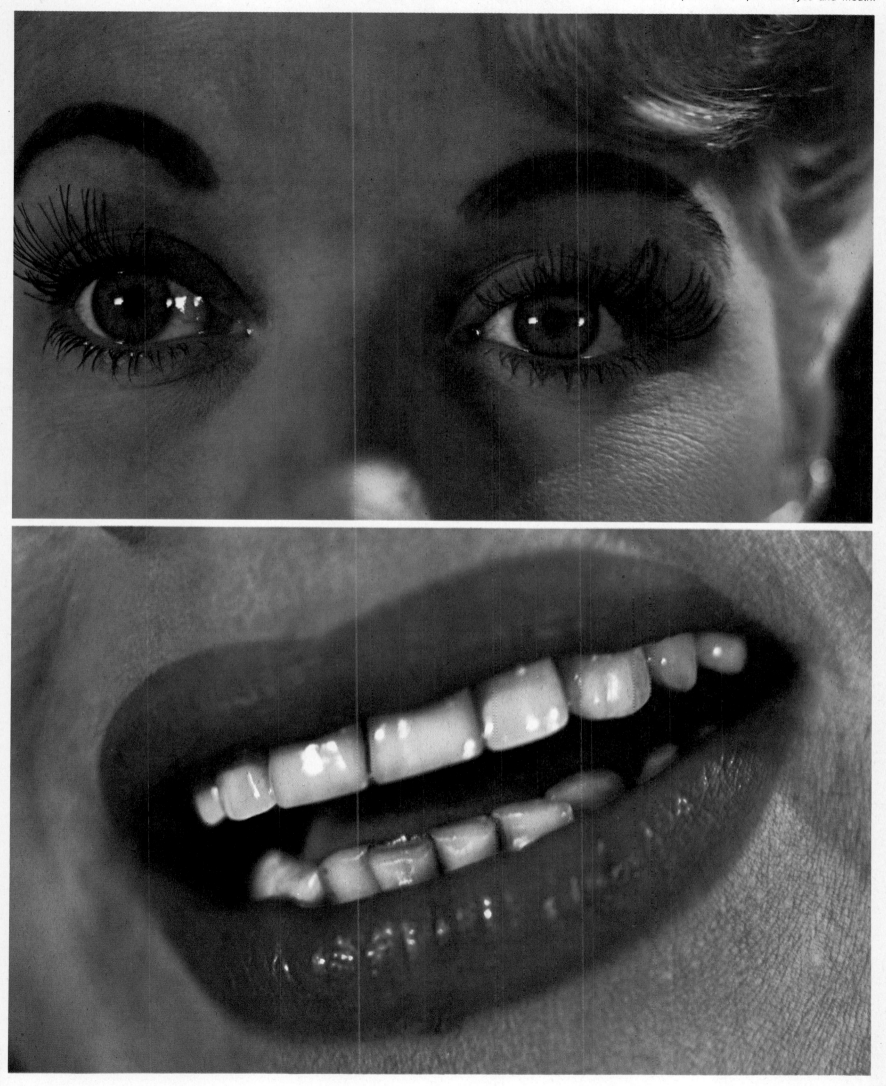

LIFE loved Lucy back in 1943. Miss Ball's coloring was so perfect that experts called her "Technicolor Tessie," as Walt Sanders proved with just her eyes and mouth.

The Starlet Factory

*For the big movie studios, the production of starlets was
a highly efficient operation. LIFE showed how it worked
in a 1948 story on the manufacture of Colleen Townsend.*

Aglow with her most confident smile, Colleen poses for a 20th Century-Fox screen-test identification photograph.

Colleen's face began to turn up in national magazines as the studio press agents opened their campaign. Here she appears as a bride on a June 1946 cover.

Teetotaler Townsend was embarrassed by this beer ad.

| JANUARY | FEBRUARY | MARCH | APRIL | MAY | JUNE |

Determined to put Colleen's face on the wall of every home, office and barracks in America all year, Fox's corps of press agents had her pose for 12 calendar pictures.

"DARLING, YOU'RE GOING PLACES!" CRIES COLUMNIST HEDDA HOPPER

The buildup's result: Colleen won the ultimate accolade, an interview with columnist Hedda Hopper, who said that she'd go far. Colleen retired in 1950 after four films.

JULY	AUGUST	SEPTEMBER	OCTOBER	NOVEMBER	DECEMBER

Photographers used a bewildering variety of props to suggest April Showers, a June wedding, Indian summer (feathers), and to make her image both sweet and seductive.

About one in every six LIFE covers, on an average, featured movie actresses (and a few actors).

Sheree North was heralded in 1955 as a new Monroe. Long years later she played character roles.

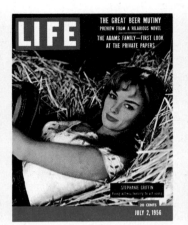

Stephanie Griffin, on a 1956 cover, made no hay in films, but did play in TV's The Great Gildersleeve.

Joan Leslie, who was Gary Cooper's sweetheart in Sergeant York (1941), danced on the cover.

Britishers Joan Elan, Dorothy Bromily and Audrey Dalton arrived big in 1952 and made it small.

Barbara Bel Geddes was praised by LIFE in 1948 as a new film star after she triumphed on the stage.

Miroslava, a Czech, played in The Brave Bulls (1950). She died in a 1955 automobile accident.

Cybill Shepherd of The Last Picture Show modeled Chinese-influenced fashions for LIFE in 1971.

Barbara Bates refused to do pin-ups but wore a swimsuit for LIFE. She was in All About Eve (1950).

Marta Toren arrived from Sweden in 1949 and was cast as an exotic. She died in 1957.

Yvette Mimieux played beach bunnies in the '60s and later wrote movie and TV scripts.

Dawn Addams got a cover in 1954 and occasional parts, then wed and divorced an Italian prince.

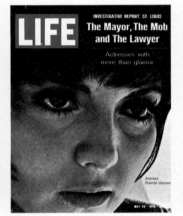

Brenda Vaccaro acted on stage (Cactus Flower, 1965), screen (Midnight Cowboy, 1969) and TV.

Ruth Roman, Kirk Douglas' girl in Champion (1949), proved she had more than looks.

Julie London had the hit record "Cry Me a River" in 1955 and two years later made it to Hollywood.

Colleen Townsend, after her big 1948 buildup (page 98), retired in 1950 to a religious life.

Ina Balin, a Brooklyn-born beauty, twinkled briefly in From the Terrace (1961) with Paul Newman.

Phyllis Kirk, a successful singer, went west for Our Very Own (1951), then returned to the cafés.

Peggy Lloyd, one of the imitators of the Three Graces on page 93, had a part in Cover Girl (1943).

Anna Maria Alberghetti sang in The Medium (1954). She resurfaced in TV commercials.

Kerima undertook the "longest movie kiss" with Trevor Howard in Outcast of the Islands (1952).

t's even possible to recognize quite a large number of them in this brief sampling.

elena Carter's 1948 cover alleged e learned how to fence opposite rol Flynn at Hunter College.

Jayne Mansfield was Hollywood's "smartest dumb blonde" in 1956. She died in a 1967 accident.

Pat Crowley won a contest to star in Forever Female (1954). She later prospered in TV comedies.

Suzy Parker, a top model of the 1950s, played opposite Cary Grant in Kiss Them For Me (1957).

Rita Gam, a siren in The Thief (1952) married in 1956 and retired to New York society.

nice Rule's fine notices in the ginal cast of Broadway's Picnic 953) got her a movie contract.

Ella Raines in 1947 had the classy looks of such other Howard Hawks finds as Lauren Bacall.

May Britt took the Dietrich role in the 1959 remake of Blue Angel. She married Sammy Davis in 1960.

Marcia Van Dyke, cousin of an M-G-M official, could sing, dance, play the violin, even act.

Elaine Stewart, an Arab princess in Hajji Baba (1954), later became a TV game show hostess.

an Rice, imported from Britain for ney's Robin Hood (1952), ended starring in horror films.

Nicole Maurey played opposite Bing Crosby, and opposite monsters in The Day of the Triffids (1963).

Jean Seberg won Otto Preminger's Joan of Arc contest in 1957 and later acted in European films.

Jane Greer caught attention modeling the WAC uniform. That led to films and a 1947 cover.

Terry Moore got wet for LIFE in 1953. She was in Mighty Joe Young (1950), and TV in the '60s.

gy Dow was a psychiatrist's se in Harvey (1950). She mar- d and retired in 1951.

Joy Lansing, another "another Monroe" in 1949, returned to a career as a theater and café vocalist.

Pier Angeli played waif-like parts but lost the lead role in Green Mansions (1959) to Audrey Hepburn.

Tuesday Weld, an offbeat beauty, attracted the editors in 1963 and an underground following later.

Lucia Bosé, Miss Italy of 1947, married topflight Spanish matador Luis Miguel Dominguín in 1955.

But Some Made It Big

It helped a buildup to have a beautiful build. But neither build nor buildup guaranteed a successful film career; that required talent, personality—and a whole lot of luck.

Lana Turner struck this period-piece pose for an early publicity picture, run with a 1940 story. From roles as the sweatered girl-next-door, she graduated to Hollywood's version of the worldly sophisticate.

Mia Farrow, daughter of "Me Jane" Maureen O'Sullivan and director John Farrow, launched her career via the TV series Peyton Place. LIFE spotted her in 1964, before she made things hum in Hollywood.

Raquel Welch's remarkable attributes had only begun to attract attention when this picture was published in 1964. What followed was one of moviedom's most spectacular publicity campaigns: she was on 108 magazine covers in the next two years.

102

As a starlet Debbie Reynolds brought to the screen a freshness and vivacity that never flagged throughout a solid career. In 1951, LIFE published this sheet of contact prints, made by Philippe Halsman, to show readers how its covers were selected. The one finally chosen for this issue appears on page 87.

By 1948 Ava Gardner had whirled into the limelight with two stormy marriages (to Mickey Rooney and Artie Shaw) and a series of adventurous roles that led to stardom in The Hucksters (1947). Still to come were Frank Sinatra and starring vehicles like Mogambo (1953) and The Barefoot Contessa (1954).

For a 1949 story on aspiring actresses, Philippe Halsman gathered eight bit players. Only one of the group eventually hit stardom. Halsman guessed she would. "She plays the camera," he reported at the time, "the way a virtuoso plays an instrument."

LOIS MAXWELL

SUZANNE DALBERT

RICK SOMA

LAURETTE LUEZ

JANE NIGH

DOLORES GARDNER

MARILYN MONROE

CATHY DOWNS

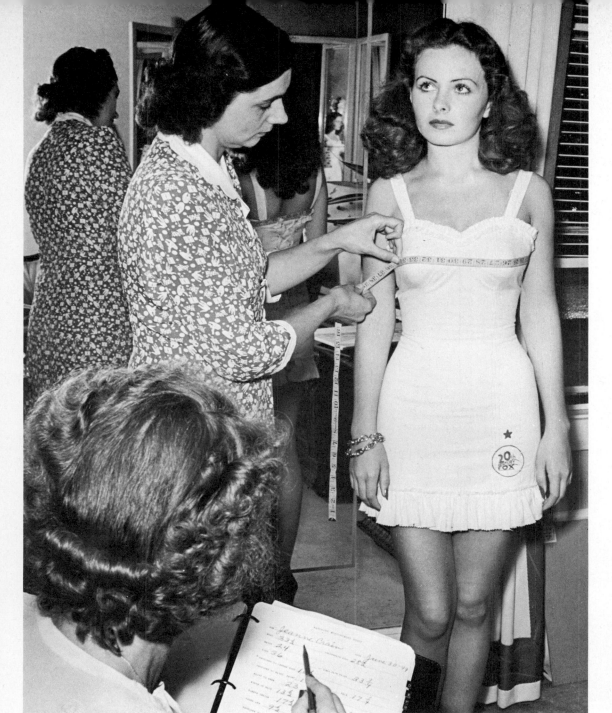

Jeanne Crain wore the studio's all-purpose underwear when she was being measured for a dress form by 20th Century-Fox wardrobe women in 1944. Her delicate beauty made her a star of the '40s.

In this 1940 cover picture of rapidly budding starlet Rita Hayworth at a picnic, she projected a rather plainer allure than she was to display a year later in her most famous photograph (page 69).

Leggy Linda Darnell was only 20 when LIFE ran this picture in 1944. She starred in Forever Amber (1947), and died in a 1965 fire at the age of 44.

A Boost for the Boys too . . .

*Young male stars got their modest portion of studio hype,
and LIFE did not dispute the public's appetite for those
handsome faces, perched, occasionally, on muscular torsos.*

*Two in an endless line of film Tarzans were the late Lex
Barker, Tarzan No. 10, and Elmo Lincoln, who was the
first Tarzan in 1918. They got together in 1949.*

In 1954, three new actors who set hearts athrob in the under-21 set—Rock Hudson, Tony Curtis and Robert Wagner (from top) were on the ladder to success.

From far-off France came the young Louis Jourdan. The problem was to teach him English, presenting the magazine with the opportunity in 1946 to show the facial contortions accompanying his English lessons.

Despite fun and games with starlets and despite the importance of a star's performance, LIFE recognized that Hollywood's essential ingredient was the film itself. Its photographers covered them on quiet sets, in noisy urban neighborhoods and in the wilderness; its editors analyzed them—and sometimes gave away the plot.

The Movies

LIFE dealt with some 800 motion pictures during the 15-plus years when "Movie of the Week" was a regular feature, plus about as many more without that editorial title. This broad coverage of movies as movies was the magazine's acknowledgment that beyond all those stories about all those stars and starlets, beyond all that talent, what finally counted was the end product in that round flat can.

The editors watched as many films being made as they could and detailed their plots in "Movie of the Week." In the magazine's zeal to inform, it even gave away the endings of suspense films. *Odd Man Out* needled the audience to a state of anxiety through the drawn-out flight of the wounded James Mason, stumbling and crawling to get away from police pursuers. In reporting on the film, LIFE also blabbed that in the end Mason and his girl friend were killed. None of this, however, seemed to have a harmful effect on the box office.

Tracing a movie's story line posed a special kind of challenge, and the magazine found many ways to meet it. One was to use candid-style photographs, shot during the actual filming, instead of the tableau-style, flashbulb-flattened publicity stills that had been the pre-LIFE standard. Musicals were, in some ways, harder to cover photographically than big dramatic films; in other ways, easier. "They run right through those dances," staff photographer Ed Clark said, "and you have to be mighty fast on the shutter release to catch them at the right instant. Fortunately, they always took about a thousand takes, too." But musicals also had advantages. "Photographing *An American in Paris* was a pleasure," Clark found, "because, like most musicals, the filming was done to prerecorded tracks, so we could move around, shoot or even sneeze, without ruining the sound. In a straight film, it's like Arnold Palmer addressing a win-or-lose putt on the last green. You worry about the click of the shutter."

LIFE not only covered *An American in Paris* but, in a small way, helped produce it. The Los Angeles bureau's photographic lab used an Eastman process that could develop color overnight faster than the studio could print its daily takes. "I'd lay out my transparencies on a light table every morning," said Clark, "and they would check their color from them."

On the other hand, covering *Porgy and Bess* taxed even LIFE's spendthrift attention, because it took 25 weeks of shooting and reshooting to get the Gershwin opera the way Sam Goldwyn wanted it. The delays were a help, however, to the almost tone-deaf star, Sidney Poitier, who devoted a month to studying his ghost-singer, the baritone Robert McFerrin, feeling the singer's jaws and neck and peering

down his throat so that he could mimic the muscular contractions when he mouthed his numbers before the camera.

Just like the rest of the world, LIFE was fascinated by Westerns. It did its share of intellectualizing about what it called "the most stylized dramatic form since Greek tragedy" and sent its photographers into the perilous midst of many a cattle or buffalo stampede (sometimes hidden in under-hoof bunkers) in the spirit of responsible photojournalism. Its photographers also, of course, faced combat hazards on all fronts in World War II, a fact that ever thereafter gave the magazine a special perspective—knowledgeable and concerned—on movies about warfare, and even made it possible for LIFE to help in the filming of some of them.

The filming of epics tended to produce spectacular problems—and spectacular picture stories—for the magazine, since shooting frequently occurred in wild or remote locations and usually with hordes of people. Covering *Lawrence of Arabia* in the Arabian desert *(pages 210-211)* was fairly typical. The going was rugged and the sand, besides being a hazard to the cameras, posed the same problem as snow does in whiteout epics: to shoot trackless desert a photographer had better be skilled at levitation or else use very long lenses.

A fertile source of anecdotes about the problems of making pictures about making movies was John Huston's *Moby Dick,* which was filmed over a span of seven months and across a good part of the north Atlantic, using as many as 20 fake whales—from small models to 60-foot floating mockups constructed of rubber, wood and steel. Erich Lessing and Carl Mydans were assigned to cover the story. The weather was consistently frightful, a good part of the cast was constantly seasick, Leo Genn was injured, Richard Basehart broke his leg, one of the whales sank, and Gregory Peck—the tempest-tossed Captain Ahab—was dunked repeatedly. "We were soaking wet most of the time," Lessing recalled. The haunting last scene, of Ahab entangled in the harpoon lines on the whale's back *(pages 188-189)* and being dragged to the bottom, was achieved by strapping Peck, complete with his fake peg leg, to a whale section that was really a massive cylinder hooked to a trawler, and motorized to roll and dip. It was shot last, for what proved to be obvious reasons. "I thought it would be a trick shot in miniature," Peck said later, "but by God if Huston didn't tie me on the side of the whale and roll me under the water!"

Nine LIFE movie covers heralded new films whose subject matter ranged from lyrical nostalgia to controversy, spectacle and double-domed philosophy.

LIFE

NEW SERIES ON A FAMILY PROBLEM:
HOW TO GIVE CHILDREN'S PARTIES
KOREA—AND HOW TRUMAN REACTED

SHIRLEY JONES
IN MOVIE 'CAROUSEL'

20 CENTS

FEBRUARY 6, 1956

LIFE

WOMEN BOWLERS
SPORTY SOCIAL WHIRL FOR EIGHT MILLION
WHAT GOLD FUSS IS ABOUT

JILL HAWORTH
AND SAL MINEO
IN 'EXODUS'

DECEMBER 12, 1960

LIFE

Her Hair Cropped,
Silvana Mangano Acts
Collaborator Role

APRIL 11, 1960

AVERAGE WEEKLY CIRCULATION 6,700,000

LIFE

MARRIAGE ON THE CAMPUS
SO YOU WANT TO HUNT URANIUM

LESLIE CARON IN 'DADDY LONG LEGS'

20 CENTS

MAY 23, 1955

LIFE

My
Secret Life
with
Bogart
by
WOODY
ALLEN

MARCH 21 · 1969 · 40¢

LIFE

FORMER PRESIDENT TRUMAN TELLS HOW
HE FIRED THE CABINET PRIMA DONNAS
MOVIE-MAKING IN THE DE MILLE MANNER

DE MILLE DIRECTS EXODUS
IN 'TEN COMMANDMENTS'

20 CENTS

OCTOBER 24, 1955

LIFE

Movie Career for Rowan and Martin
From Laugh-In
To Scare-In

MAY 23 · 1969 · 40¢

LIFE

CHICAGO City of Exciting
New Skyscrapers
Intrigue behind the Spy Swap
'FORBIDDEN' FILMS
A FAMILY DILEMMA

SHIRLEY
MacLAINE
Tortured Role
in
A Daring Movie

ALSO THIS WEEK

Blazing Night Life
of Japan
12 Color Pages
by Eliot Elisofon

Sonny Liston
Meanest Fighter,
Maybe Next Champ

Way Up Way of Living
on California's Cliffs

FEBRUARY 23 · 1962 · 20¢

LIFE

U.S. GAMBLING MOB IN CUBA
NEW UPSETS ON A TROUBLED ISLAND

A CAMERA MASTERPIECE:
DRAMA AND MOOD ON A CITY STREET

YUL BRYNNER IN MOVIE,
'BROTHERS KARAMAZOV'

MARCH 10, 1958 25 CENTS

Musicals

Movie musicals, the happiest and most colorful of films, were a genre all their own. Stars, chorus kids and even cartoon characters leaped at the chance to appear in them.

Only a year after the first squawks from Jack Warner's Vitaphone contraption—the Edison recording device that in 1926 gave films a voice—Al Jolson was down on his knees singing "Mammy" in *The Jazz Singer.* From that audibly auspicious moment on, music was seldom absent from the sound track.

In the earliest of the talkies, sound was sometimes an afterthought; musical scores were recorded chiefly to provide a background for otherwise silent dramas. But by the early '30s, theater marquees and billboards were proclaiming full-fledged *All Talking! All Singing! All Dancing!* movies.

These Depression musicals were exemplified by the Busby Berkeley spectacle: a flimsy backstage tale was used as an excuse to string lively tunes, tap dancing and chorines' precision performances together into larger-than-life set pieces. Gradually the Berkeley style of production gave way to more sophisticated comedy, some of it trickling down from Broadway, and this in turn was replaced by the patriotic rousers of the war years and finally the big blockbusters of the '50s and '60s: *Oklahoma!, South Pacific, Guys and Dolls, West Side Story* and *Funny Girl.*

An enduring subspecies of the stage and screen musicals was the "backstage" classic, in which the humble chorus girl achieves stardom and success. This genre also evolved with the times. Its early, simple form was exemplified by *42nd Street,* in which Ruby Keeler stepped into the leading lady's dancing shoes. It had developed considerably by the '60s, when backstagers like the Broadway-born *Gypsy* and *Funny Girl* took the behind-the-scenes musical about as far as it could go in complexity.

The Hollywood musical presented LIFE with a problem: how to set forth all this music and movement on paper. In the sixth week after the magazine's arrival on the scene in 1936, LIFE attempted to capture music's rhythm with a picture sequence on the dance. Accompanying an article on popular dances of the day was an animated spread on Fred Astaire, which reproduced, step by step, one of his most imaginative and highly calisthenic tap routines. As the musicals became more sophisticated, so did LIFE's coverage, progressing from panels of dance steps to wide-angle, full-color supershows, photographed on the set by such expert lensmen as Gjon Mili and Henry Groskinsky.

They had their problems. When Mili was photographing *Guys and Dolls* (1955), for example, the palmy days were fading fast. A hard-working still photographer had to set up where he could on stages crowded with camera and sound equipment, harassed crews, and preoccupied and occasionally resentful actors and directors. "Although I was part of the crew myself," says Mili, who was working for producer Samuel Goldwyn at the time, "I had to be ready to take the right photograph at the right moment from the right angle—or lose the shot forever."

Sometimes the project was even dangerous. Henry Groskinsky, photographing *Camelot* (1967), risked life and limb getting a head-on shot of a knight bearing down, lance at the ready. "I was using a telephoto lens," says Groskinsky, "and didn't look up until horse and rider were right on top of me. That spear missed my head by 10 inches at most. Too close for me."

But the results were worth the highly synchronized effort and even the risk. For in capturing not only the costumes and the color but also the movement of the big shows, they caught the spirit of their music as well.

"Take back your mink from whence it came!" screech the Hot Box chorines in Sam Goldwyn's version of Broadway's musical, Guys and Dolls (1955).

111

Her fringe flying, Janet Leigh swings aloft with the help of friends in Bye Bye Birdie (1962). "It'll be a long time before I do another musical," she said then.

High as the flag on the Fourth of July, Nurse Nellie For-
bush (Mitzi Gaynor) joins in a special South Pacific picture act that appeared in 1958.

Spread-eagled against a fiery background in a defiant
leap, Russ Tamblyn announces in West Side Story
(1961) that his gang members rule his world.

Teetering on his heels, sailor Gene Kelly is supported
by his anxious dance partner, the Mouse King, in a fan-
tasy sequence from Anchors Aweigh (1945) that mixed
live action with animated drawings.

Hollywood's most popular dancer, Fred Astaire drew this comment after his screen test: "Can't act. Can't sing. Can dance a little." Here, in a "Puttin' on the Ritz" number in Blue Skies (1946), he proves that the last part of the assessment, at least, was sound.

Doing a typical hoofing duet called the "Shorty George" in You Were Never Lovelier (1942), Rita Hayworth is as lovely, and Astaire as effortlessly graceful, as ever. This was their second film together.

The classic Astaire, in formal dress and with his classic partner Ginger Rogers, sweeps through the airborne finale of a dance called "The Yam" in Carefree (1938). They made 10 movies together.

Astaire and Judy Garland masquerade as a couple of tramps in Easter Parade (1948). Astaire, called out of premature retirement as a last-minute replacement for Gene Kelly, took the part as a favor to Kelly, who had injured his ankle in practice.

Reacting to the unearthly beauty of Stupefyin' Jones ▶ (Julie Newmar), the ''inhoomin'' Scragg boys are elevated to attitudes ranging from awe to angst in this everybody-up impression of Li'l Abner (1959).

''June Is Bustin' Out All Over'' amid a swirl of petticoats and bloomers as dancers filming Carousel (1956) are tossed head over heels.

The very picture of richly rewarded wickedness, high-rolling Sportin' Life (Sammy Davis) struts out the cyn-ical It Ain't Necessarily So at a church picnic in the movie of Gershwin's Porgy and Bess (1959).

Yul Brynner, as Siam's king in Rodgers and Hammerstein's The King and I (1956), sings a song of puzzlement. A fine photographer, Brynner himself took the stills that were used in LIFE's coverage.

Kicking up dust against a lowering sky, dancing cowboys have a brawl in a dream sequence of Oklahoma! (1955), the widescreen filming of the 1943 stage hit. LIFE lauded the Agnes De Mille dances as being part of the plot instead of an interruption.

Betty Grable, the song-and-dance queen of the 1940s, takes a chorus-girl bow while dancing to ''When You Wore a Tulip'' in Tin Pan Alley (1940).

A flapper chorus reacts to a gangland killing in The Best Things in Life Are Free (1956).

Eve (Shirley MacLaine) has just eaten the apple in Cole Porter's version of Eden during

Ann Miller, as shrew Kate's kid sister in Kiss Me, Kate (1953), makes the skirts fly to the tune of "Tom, Dick or Harry."

a dance in Can-Can (1960). The movie evoked the flavor of 19th Century Paris.

In front of a Dufy-like background, Gene Kelly dances as An American in Paris (1951).

121

Leggy Juliet Prowse aims a kick at the sky in G.I. Blues (1960). She impressed Nikita Khrushchev when he visited the Can-Can set in 1959.

Going right to the top in her first film, Funny Girl (1968), Barbra Streisand parodies Swan Lake, flapping upward as she is hauled by a wired harness.

Warming up for the big take-off, Natalie Wood practices for her striptease in Gypsy (1962). She rehearsed for a month, and finally did so well, LIFE reported, that Gypsy Rose Lee herself, watching her on the set, burst into tears of nostalgia.

Westerns

From the earliest Westerns, around 1900, to the horse operas of the 1950s, the same plot line drew the fans in multitudes: the mandatory triumph of virtue over evil.

Since 1903, when Edwin S. Porter filmed *The Great Train Robbery* in the badlands of New Jersey, movie Westerns have become, to the whole world, the archetypal American folk opera. John Florea, photographing *Yellow Sky* for LIFE in 1949, analyzed this enduring appeal: "They could get away with anything —shooting, floozies, every vice known to man. And the mores and morals were so well defined—everything broke down into white hats versus black hats." With a few notable exceptions, the white hats always won.

The first of the good guys was "Broncho Billy" Anderson, a phlegmatic ex-vaudevillian from Little Rock, who starred in a series of silent Westerns that set the pattern for almost all "oaters" to come: the villains deep-dyed, the hero a paragon, the heroine hardly noticeable. By 1914, William S. Hart had bent the pattern, but he couldn't break it. Hart, a stickler for realism, played a "good bad guy" in surroundings that reeked of horseflesh, redeye, sagebrush, dust, and a minimum of fakery. But by the early '20s, the public had had enough of reality, and cast Bill Hart aside for Tom Mix, hero of a West that never was, who righted all wrongs without getting a smudge on his white suit.

From Mix in the silents, it was only a short step to the singing cowboy hero of the talking '30s and '40s. Roy Rogers, with his horse Trigger, his steady cowgirl Dale Evans and his sidekick Gabby Hayes, helped make the Wild West the home of country-and-western music —as did fellow yodelers Gene Autry and Tex Ritter. Rogers was a farm boy from Ohio, Autry hated to ride and Ritter was a former law student. But rural and small-town audiences flocked to the movie houses during the Depression and World War II to hear them sing plaintively of broken hearts and sagebrush romance. The audiences also admired the uncannily intelligent horses and chuckled at folksy sidekicks like Andy Devine—in the tradition, which few movie-goers recognized, of Don Quixote and Sancho Panza.

The epic Western hit the screen with *The Covered Wagon* (1923) and *Cimarron* (1931). To the formula of bad guy against good guy was added another: How the West Was Won, with grand, sweeping views of American history often only loosely bound together by visual truth. And from time to time a maverick raised its head: George Marshall's rowdy version of *Destry Rides Again* (1939), John Ford's landmark *Stagecoach* (1939) and his anti-Western, *The Man Who Shot Liberty Valance* (1962). But such occasional exceptions only proved the rule, and the classic Hollywood Western of the '30s and '40s remained as stylized as a morality play.

Not until the early '50s did glimpses of gritty reality appear with any consistency. Alan Ladd in the "psychological" *Shane* (1953) was an unkempt drifter; Indians resembled people in *Broken Arrow* (1950). By the '60s, the classic Western was barely recognizable under its coat of realistic prairie dust. A steady trend toward more violence was evident in such films as Sam Peckinpah's *The Wild Bunch* (1969). And foreign imitations, especially the so-called Spaghetti Westerns that were made in Italy in the later 1960s, added an exotic touch of their own.

But the golden formula, however much tarnished, still showed through. John Wayne, the last and one of the best, carried on the tradition. The Western hero's face was seamier, his white hat grimy, his character smudged. But he still rode into the sunset, leaving the thankful settlers and the rueful floozie to wonder, "Who *was* that lonesome stranger?"

Roy Rogers was king of the singing cowboys in the 1940s. Astride his performing palomino wonder horse, Trigger, he is the picture of the pure, honest—and unreal—Western hero of his time. Of him it was said, "He could kiss his horse but never the heroine."

Good Guys and Bad Guys

In the classic screen shoot-'em-up it was never a problem to distinguish hero from villain: his hat was the right color—and besides, he was (and usually wore) the star.

Bill Hart was black-hatted but often did good dee

Marshal Will Kane, the last brave (and honest) man in town, stalks down an empty street to confront the villains at High Noon (1952). The hero of this classic Western: Gary Coop

"Another redskin bites the dust," said LIFE of this scene from John Ford's realistic Western, Stagecoach (1939).

urt Lancaster is okay in Gunfight at the OK Corral (1957).   Alan Ladd is triumphant as a good guy in Shane (1953).

Bill Boyd was good guy Hopalong Cassidy despite his hat.   Ex-bad guy Gregory Peck opens fire in Gunfighter (1950).

utlaw Tyrone Power pays the price in Jesse James (1939).   Good guy John Wayne belts his stepson, Montgomery Clift, in Red River (1948), an early Oedipus-complex Western.

The Not-so-Good Guys

When the time-tested formula for oaters finally wore thin, moviemakers domestic and foreign tried a number of new twists—everything from sadism to outright parody.

A battered Clint Eastwood looks down the muzzle of a ▶ bad guy's pistol in A Fistful of Dollars (1964). Eastwood exchanged his clean-cut image, formed on television's Rawhide, for that of a brutal gunman in Italian-made ''Spaghetti Westerns.''

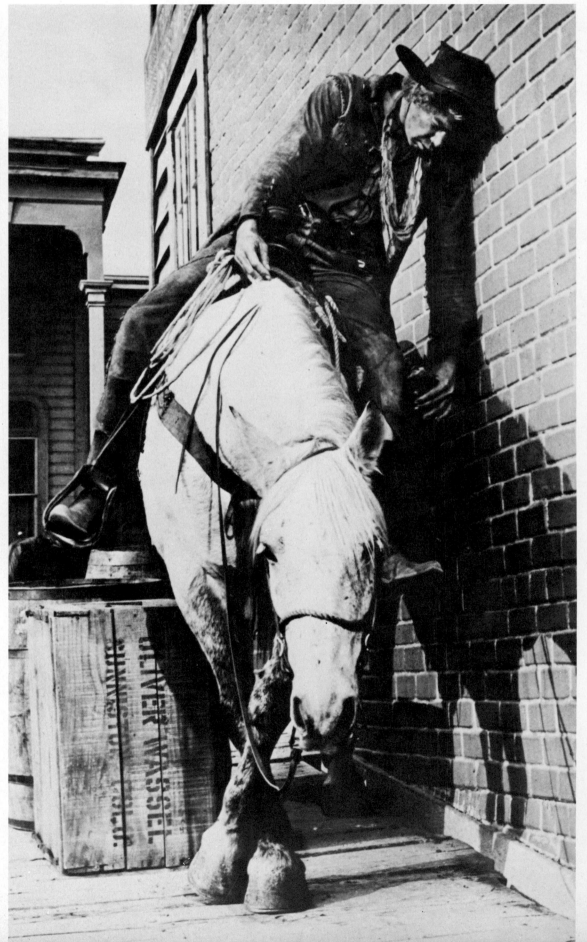

Bruce Dern, as a psychopathic killer, glowers in Mark Rydell's The Cowboys (1972), an offbeat Western in which hero John Wayne is killed, while his youthful side-kicks win out in the final frames.

A sozzled Lee Marvin and his horse both collapse in Cat Ballou (1965), a milestone comic ''anti-Western.'' Marvin played two roles, the good—if drunken—Kid Shelleen and his no-good twin brother.

By the time John Wayne (below, left) got around to fighting it out in the Hollywood-made mud of McLintock (1963), the white-hat image had pretty well faded from the picture.

Women in Westerns

The heroines of the silents and the early talkies were principally ornaments, but in the Westerns of later years they asserted themselves with guns and even fists.

Marilyn Monroe, a dude rancher in The Misfits (1960), discovers the horse Clark Gable is roping will be made into dog food and angrily tries to stop him.

Jane Russell gave pin-up pictures like this one for *The Outlaw* (1941) to GIs everywhere, becoming the unofficial "queen of the motionless pictures."

Out of type—drenched, disheveled and pistol-packing —Marlene Dietrich exhibits her courage as Frenchy in Destry Rides Again *(1939).*

As a slightly different Frenchie, in 1950's Frenchie, *Shelley Winters plays a sexy gambling hall girl with a heart of gold. But she never got kissed.*

131

Drama and Melodrama

*The human condition was examined from every angle
in films that were instructive, destructive, brimming with
life and love, or saturated with all kinds of violence.*

Drama was the great staple of the movies. Depending on the director, Hollywood was as much at home with the serious achievements of Broadway as with its homemade melodramas and scenarios of suspense and romance.

Not infrequently, the drama on the set was equal to that of the script. When quadruple threat Orson Welles came to Hollywood, he had a four-way contract with RKO, as producer, scriptwriter, director and actor. LIFE reported that Welles was so determined to run his own show with no meddling from the brass that, when he spied two RKO executives arriving unannounced on the set of *Citizen Kane,* he called off shooting for the day and organized a baseball game among his company. He resumed work later, when the execs were back at the head office screaming about that madman Welles who was wasting RKO money—on what became a film classic.

The power of drama sometimes derived from human stresses that made brutal physical demands on the performers themselves. Anne Bancroft found herself engaged in near-brawls in two of her movies: as the teacher of rebellious young Helen Keller in *The Miracle Worker* and as the angry wife of Peter Finch in *The Pumpkin Eater.* In the latter film she and Finch fought for two and a half days in order to provide a 45-second sequence.

On occasion, dramatic power flowed from the very pairing of the stars. The special chemistry between John Garfield and Lana Turner converted their roles in *The Postman Always Rings Twice* into personifications of evil fed by lust. On the other hand, audiences were moved to almost unbearable anguish when the romantic combination of Ingrid Bergman and Charles Boyer was sundered by the Nazis in *Arch of Triumph.* And some scripted pairings worked so well that they

were transferred to real life: Humphrey Bogart and Lauren Bacall made four films together and imitated art by getting married.

Despite the occasional mixture of many elements in dramatic films, it became possible to draw a distinction between the two basic kinds of what was generally called The Thriller. Some, particularly in later years, were outright wallowings in violence, but others were fine-honed studies in suspense. The acknowledged expert at the latter was Alfred Hitchcock. In a 1959 interview with Herbert Brean, a LIFE staff writer and a mystery novelist himself, the old master let the reading audience in on a few of his cliff-hanger secrets.

"The trouble with suspense is that few people know what it is," he told Brean. "Let me illustrate. Let us suppose that three men are sitting in a room in which a ticking bomb has been planted. It is going to go off in 10 minutes. The audience does not know it is there, and the men do not know it is there either. So they go on talking inanely of the weather or yesterday's baseball game. After 10 minutes of desultory conversation the bomb goes off. What is the result? The unsuspecting audience gets a surprise. One surprise. That's all.

"Suppose," Hitchcock continued, "the story were told differently. This time while the men still do not know the bomb is there, the audience does know. The men still talk inanities, but now the most banal thing they say is charged with excitement. The audience wants them to get out of the room, but they talk on, and when one finally says 'Let's leave,' the entire audience is praying for them to do so. But another man says, 'No, wait a minute, I want to finish my coffee,' and the audience yearns for them to leave.

"That," said Hitchcock—and here he broke off for a Hitchcockian pause—"is suspense."

*In his first film, Citizen Kane (1941), Orson Welles
played a newspaper tycoon who tried to bully his way
into the governor's mansion. He also co-authored the
script and directed and produced the film.*

133

Broadway on Celluloid

Making a play into a movie was a standard Hollywood exercise, and though the results varied, the camera sometimes proved better than flesh-and-blood reality.

Terror—stimulated by the sound of Gestapo footsteps below—immobilizes Jewish refugees hiding on the top floor of an Amsterdam warehouse in the movie version of The Diary of Anne Frank (1959). To reinforce their mood of jittery apprehension, director George Stevens startled the cast by firing blanks.

Using a montage of two photographs, Gordon Parks showed simultaneously the opposite reactions of Paul Newman and Geraldine Page in the film based on Tennessee Williams' Sweet Bird of Youth (1962) as they get the news that the aging actress portrayed by Miss Page has made a glorious comeback.

Mildred Dunnock, as the long-suffering wife of Arthur Miller's protagonist, Willy Loman, in Death of a Salesman (1951), kneels at her husband's grave to ask his forgiveness for not being able to cry.

Karen Balkin whispers a lie about two of her teachers to her shocked grandmother, Fay Bainter, in the 1962 remake of Lillian Hellman's The Children's Hour. As in the stage original, the lie concerned lesbianism—unlike a 1936 film version that nervously substituted a conventional heterosexual triangle.

The Clinch

On deserted beaches and desert sands, in Paris and Smalltown, U.S.A.—anywhere under the sun or the moon —the flowering of romance set the cameras rolling.

Rudolph Valentino's leer at Agnes Ayres drew snickers from the audiences when the 1921 sand-blasted love story, The Sheik, was revived in 1938.

Under a Paris moon, Charles Boyer, a refugee surgeon, and Ingrid Bergman, a rootless nightclub singer, find solace in love in Arch of Triumph (1948).

Playing a cavalry sergeant turned policeman, Jim Brown, a professional football player turned actor, makes close contact with Raquel Welch, playing a fiery Mexican revolutionary, in 100 Rifles (1969).

After a slow buildup, Lauren Bacall and Humphrey Bogart kiss in To Have and Have Not (1944). To LIFE, the real explosion was Bacall: "the sulky-looking girl who saunters with catlike grace."

Lana Turner and John Garfield grapple on the beach in The Postman Always Rings Twice (1946). At first considered too hot to handle, the James M. Cain novel languished for 12 years on M-G-M's back shelf.

Hearts and Flowers

Plucking on the heartstrings of America with motion pictures awash in sentiment, frustration and brave suffering, the producers cried all the way to the bank.

Jane Wyman, as a deaf and mute farm girl in Johnny Belinda (1948), recites a prayer in sign language over the body of her murdered father. Her acting, abetted by earplugs, earned her an Oscar.

Groping through the world of silent darkness, Patty Duke as the young Helen Keller in The Miracle Worker (1962) portrays the real-life heroine whose triumphant struggle outrivaled any of those in fiction.

Personifying the common man, Gary Cooper finds his crusade against the evils of society in Frank Capra's Meet John Doe (1941) cruelly terminated by a mob slinging wet newspapers. Capra's high regard for the average citizen was reciprocated—his name on a film had the pull of a star's.

James Stewart (above), playing a hard-luck small-town bank manager in It's a Wonderful Life (1946), returns to his wife (Donna Reed) and four children after being persuaded not to kill himself.

Bette Davis, the victim of an unhappy love affair and the mother of an illegitimate child, listens with pained resignation, in The Old Maid (1939), to the reproaches of her self-righteous cousin Miriam Hopkins.

Foreign directors focused on the realistic, earthy details of everyday life and cut much of

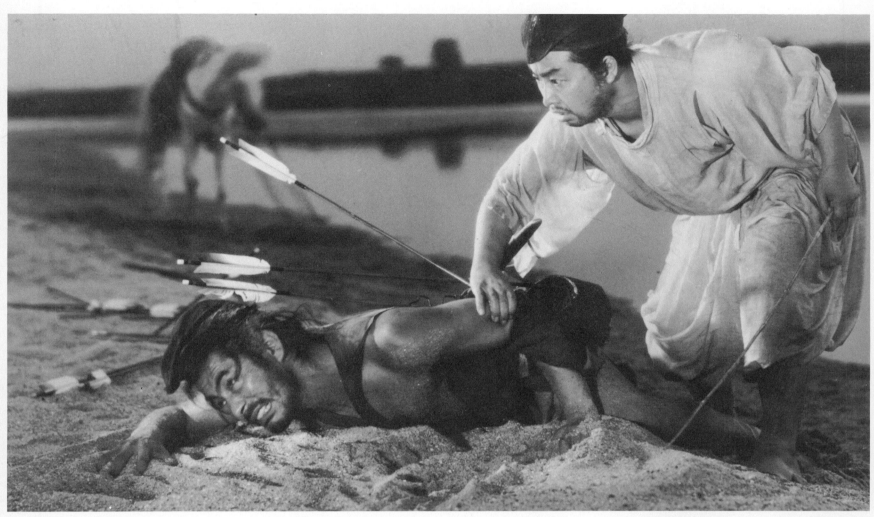

Toshiro Mifune plays a bandit being caught and subdued by the police in Kurosawa's classic Rashomon (1951). The movie presented three viewpoints of the same killing.

David Hemmings photographs a writhing Veruschka in Antonioni's Blow-Up (1967).

Marcello Mastroianni tries a new dance step during an orgy in La Dolce Vita (1961).

the gloss—and cost—from moviemaking by filming in the streets and featuring unknowns.

Sophia Loren, kept pregnant to stay out of jail, burgeons in De Sica's Yesterday, Today and Tomorrow (1964).

Unknowns were in De Sica's The Bicycle Thief (1949).

A priest is executed in Rossellini's Open City (1946).

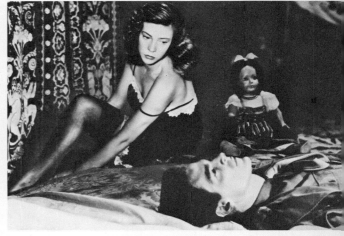

A yank meets an Italian prostitute in Paisan (1948).

Jean Seberg busses Belmondo in Breathless (1961).

Giulietta Masina is a clown in Fellini's La Strada (1956).

A young bootblack lands in jail in Shoeshine (1947).

Suspense and Violence

*From the finely honed art of apprehension to the blunt
cruelty of explicit violence, the makers of movies
became adept at appealing to the worst in the best of us.*

British-born Sidney Greenstreet, Hollywood's bulky master of menace, bears down on a victim *(Geraldine Fitzgerald)* in *Three Strangers* (1946).

James Stewart is startled as he snags his hand on the ▶
fangs of a stuffed tiger in a taxidermist's shop in *Hitchcock's The Man Who Knew Too Much* (1956).

Joan Crawford makes a trembling telephone call for ▶
help after escaping from her sister *(Bette Davis)* who is
trying literally to frighten her to death in *What Ever Happened to Baby Jane?* (1962).

Until the final moments of Gaslight (1944), audiences were unsure whether Ingrid Bergman would cut her husband, Charles Boyer, loose or cut him up.

After a savage beating in Champion (1949), Kirk Douglas goes berserk in his dressing room and smashes his hand before dying of a stroke.

Under siege after a revolt of inmates, one of the prisoners in The Birdman of Alcatraz (1962) doubles up as he catches a blast from a guard's gun.

Double-crossed by a girl, Burt Lancaster smashes a ▶ window during a suicide attempt in The Killers (1946). The film, based on Hemingway's short story, marked Lancaster's first appearance in movies.

In Dirty Harry (1971) Clint Eastwood, playing a maverick San Francisco detective, goes down shooting as he hits the California sand. With violence as his trademark, Eastwood was a box-office favorite for half a decade and the No. 1 draw in 1972.

The Naked City (1948) opens with a blonde being chloroformed and strangled by two thugs. LIFE said that the film ''comes close to being a superb movie simply because its manhunt . . . was photographed where the story takes place,'' all over Manhattan.

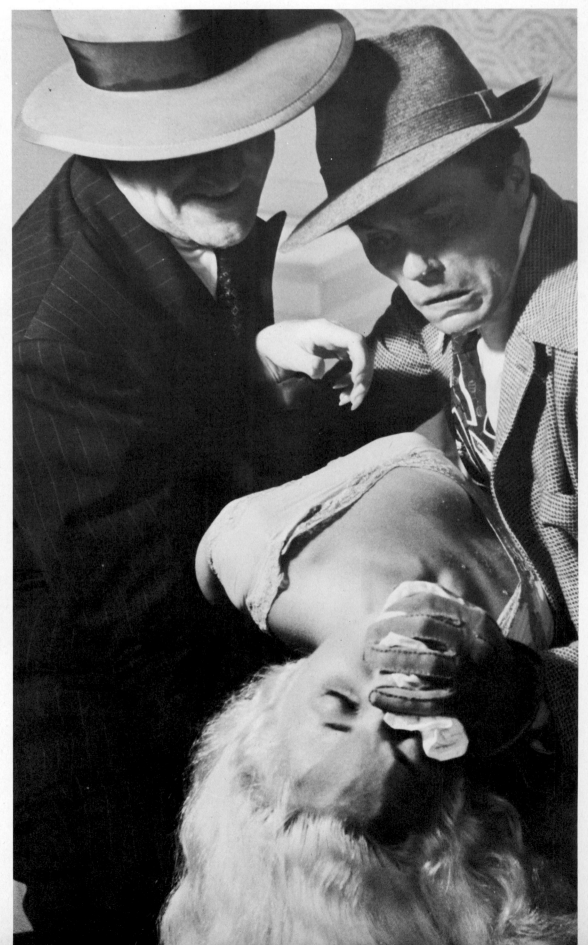

A Gestapo torturer turns a blowtorch on a leader of the Italian underground, in Roberto Rossellini's Open City (1946), in an attempt to get him to talk.

Ambushed at a highway toll booth, Sonny Corleone (James Caan) winds up a ketchup-spattered mafioso in the box-office champion, The Godfather (1972), based on Mario Puzo's best-selling novel.

Violence is made almost lyrical in a slow-motion sequence at the end of Bonnie and Clyde (1967) as Bonnie (Faye Dunaway) twitches and jerks with terrible grace under a deadly rain of bullets.

Her body gilded from head to toe, Shirley Eaton dies of skin suffocation in Goldfinger (1964), which pitted James Bond against a porcine modern Midas.

His life slowly ebbing through a bullet hole, James Mason, an IRA fugitive, painfully drags himself through the alleys of Belfast to escape police in Carol Reed's suspenseful Odd Man Out (1947).

Some Memorable Monsters

Filmdom's freaks, the most outstanding examples of the make-up department's imagination, stalked, shambled and slithered into the hearts of shuddering movie-goers.

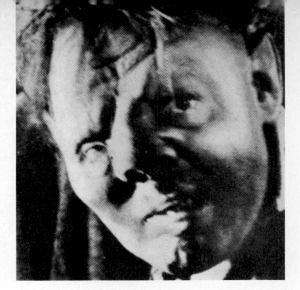

Charles Laughton's Hunchback of Notre Dame (1939) was so hideous that no publicity pictures were permitted. LIFE smuggled this one from the set.

James Cagney's Hunchback was part of his impersonation of Lon Chaney as Quasimodo in the film Man of a Thousand Faces (1957).

Rising from the watery depths of the Amazon, Ben Chapman as the Gill-Man—half man, half fish—carries the bathing-suited Julie Adams to his underwater grotto in Creature from the Black Lagoon (1954).

The Italian actor Fanfulla becomes Vernacchio, the grotesque comic of Nero's day, in Federico Fellini's phantasmagoric interpretation of Petronius' Satyricon (1969), with a cast of a thousand freaks.

A huge, glassy Cyclopean eye stares unblinkingly from the massive forehead of Polyphemus, played by Umberto Silvestri, an Italian wrestler, in Ulysses (1955). It did, that is, until Ulysses (athletically portrayed by Kirk Douglas) gouged it out with a hot log.

Nothing But the Tooth

Every melodrama worth its sweat included the climactic close-up of the open-mouthed, ear-piercing howl of anguish, fright, or frustration. It kept the audience awake.

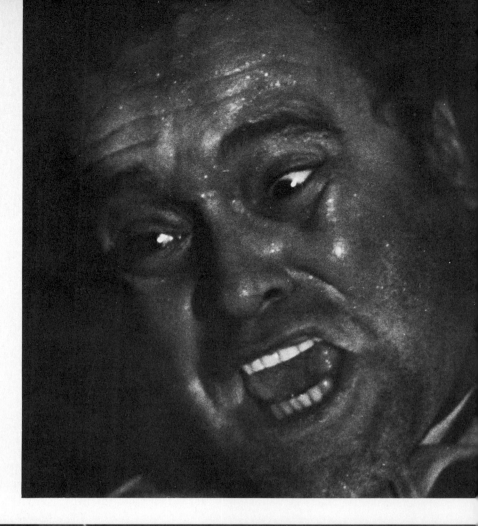

Jack Lemmon, the desperate drunk of Days of Wine and Roses (1963), looses the scream of a man possessed by the DTs after his worst bender.

From his Berlin detention cell, William Holden howls in helpless agony as he sees the woman he loves go before a Nazi firing squad in The Counterfeit Traitor (1962). His cry was drowned out by gunfire.

Taunted for being unmasculine, John Kerr cries out hysterically in the film version of Tea and Sympathy (1956).

As the long-suffering housewife in The Pumpkin Eater (1964), Anne Bancroft shrills with the fury of a bobcat as she lights into her philandering husband.

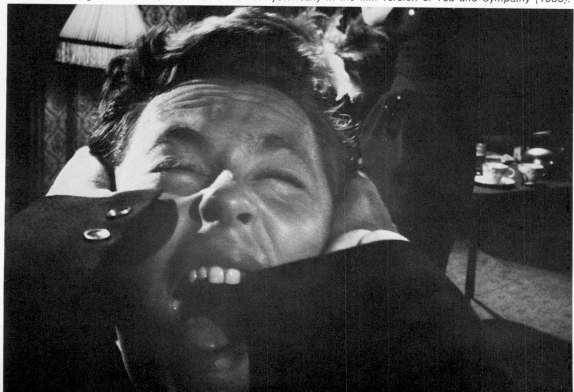

War Pictures

In its search for combat authenticity, Hollywood often sought the assistance of actors and directors—and LIFE photographers—who had authentic battle experience.

In the movies, as in life and LIFE, nothing could exceed the raw drama of war. Collaboration was, presumably, foreordained. Besides covering war films, the magazine's photographers often made a contribution to the movies' productions: not only their experience but also their photographs were useful. Robert Capa's pictures of the Spanish Civil War, for example, were used by his friend Ernest Hemingway in advising Hollywood on the filming of *For Whom the Bell Tolls.*

Not surprisingly, the best war movies were made by and with veterans of the armed services. The earliest outstanding example was the actor-director Erich von Stroheim, who had served with the Austrian cavalry before World War I and had learned to project the perfect Prussian. He was publicized as "the man you love to hate," and he became such an object of opprobrium in the '20s that people insulted him in the street and threw rolls at him in restaurants.

Meanwhile, other veterans had joined Hollywood's ranks and drew on their combat experience to bring greater authenticity to the celluloid battles. *Wings* (1927), co-winner of the first Academy Award, was the work of a trio of former World War I fliers: John Monk Saunders, who wrote it; William Wellman, who directed it; and Richard Grace, who risked and fractured his neck in it as a stunt man.

During World War II, Hollywood actors and actresses who did not actually enter the armed forces found themselves serving in military movies. In 1942 alone, 80 films touched on war in some way. The subject was not only commercial but also offered incomparable advantages as a psychological tool: *The North Star,* which was later retitled *Armored Attack,* promoted the image of the Russians as invaluable allies of the anti-Communist United States; and *In Which We Serve* glorified the achievements of the British Navy.

World War II ended, but war movies did not fade away. The popular columns of combat correspondent Ernie Pyle were converted —by the same William Wellman who had directed *Wings*—into a movie titled *The Story of G.I. Joe* (1945), one of the most realistic war movies ever made. Inclusion in the script of combat film footage and firsthand accounts of battles gave the production a raw honesty, which was authenticated by such consultants as Ernie Pyle himself and nine fellow correspondents, including LIFE's Robert Landry.

When World War II's most decorated American hero, infantryman Audie Murphy, came home, the July 16, 1945, issue of the magazine ran his picture on the cover. Seeing it, actor James Cagney invited the handsome, real-life Medal of Honor winner to Hollywood. Murphy acted—if that is the word—in a few films, to mixed reviews. Then, in 1955, he played himself in an autobiographical movie *To Hell and Back.* In the movie's recounting of his best friend's death, Murphy recalled, "We changed the part where he died in my arms. That was the way it had really happened, but it looked too corny."

Not only did the war movies flourish, but war veterans, allied and enemy alike, refought their battles on film. In 1968, revisiting the theater where a quarter of a century earlier they had both fought for their countries, ex-Marine Lee Marvin and Toshiro Mifune, a former Japanese petty officer, locked horns on a Pacific island in a private movie war titled *Hell in the Pacific.* For some time Marvin resisted the film's nonviolent ending, which called for him simply to walk away from Mifune. Even after all those years, director John Boorman told a LIFE reporter, "His instinct was to kill."

Exhausted, dirty and half crippled after days of combat at Bastogne, James Whitmore, the tough sergeant of Battleground (1949), blinks at the emerging sun, which brings promise of airborne support.

Kirk Douglas as the French Colonel Dax recoils at the sight of dead soldiers from his regiment who were ordered on a suicidal mission by an ambitious commander. This grisly antimilitaristic motion picture, Paths of Glory (1957), was made by Stanley Kubrick from an earlier best-selling novel.

In The Red Badge of Courage (1951), a frightened farm boy in a Union Army uniform (Audie Murphy) bolts at the sight of charging Confederates. As the recruit in the film from Stephen Crane's classic, Murphy, a true-life war hero, muffed his lines because he couldn't admit to fear—even in a Civil War movie.

In the 1927 silent movie Wings, the aerial combat classic that launched him, Gary Cooper casually takes leave of his friends to practice "a few figure eights before dinner." Seconds later, the shadows of two planes colliding filled the screen, and his buddies were left to pack up the dead flier's belongings.

World War I pilot Errol Flynn, killed on a suicide mission in the 1938 remake of The Dawn Patrol, expires in the cockpit. Richard Barthelmess had played the role in 1930 and by 1963 the image of the heroic pilot dying in his "crate" had become such a cliché that LIFE and Jack Lemmon spoofed it (page 253).

Erich von Stroheim, the ramrod-backed German officer of uncounted World War I films, had become a more sympathetic character, according to LIFE, when he made his Hollywood comeback as Field Marshal Erwin Rommel in Five Graves to Cairo (1943).

As the driven British colonel commanding fellow POWs in The Bridge on the River Kwai (1957), Alec Guinness won the Oscar for Best Actor.

Burgess Meredith got the part of Ernie Pyle when the columnist modestly stayed out of The Story of G.I. Joe (1945), based on his war correspondence.

Keir Dullea gave a moving performance as the taut young GI in The Thin Red Line (1964), the story of a private's baptism of fire at Guadalcanal.

William Holden was the con man of Stalag 17 (1953), whose fellow POWs beat him when they suspected him of informing. He got an Oscar for the role.

In To Hell and Back (1955), based on his autobiography, Audie Murphy stands in the turret of a flaming tank and holds off an attack by two German infantry companies. He played himself and re-created his **World War II** Medal of Honor exploits.

Lashed to a tree, mud-covered Lee Marvin glares at his captor in Hell in the Pacific (1969). Marvin, a former Marine in real life, had the role of a downed U.S. Marine flier who played brutal hide-and-seek with a Japanese officer on a tropical atoll.

Russians set their homes on fire as invading Nazi troops roll into their village in Lewis Milestone's The North Star (1943). LIFE called the film a "tone poem" whose real hero, the village itself, symbolized an entire nation's struggle against the enemy.

Survivors from a torpedoed liner rush to balance their wave-tossed vessel in Hitchcock's Lifeboat (1944). The film drew audience criticism because the Nazi skipper, his submarine also sunk in the action, seemed to be the only competent person in the cast.

Clark Gable, relinquishing command because of injuries, listens to his executive officer Burt Lancaster bark orders in Run Silent, Run Deep (1958).

Noel Coward (foreground) and shipmates cling to a raft in In Which We Serve (1942).

Bogart, as Captain Queeg, cowers in the wheelhouse in The Caine Mutiny (1954).

Comedies

Employing an amalgam of serious analysis and madcap invention, many talents worked hard—and successfully— at the art of sending the movie-goers home laughing.

The world is a comedy to those who think, a tragedy to those who feel. Moviemakers who had never heard of Horace Walpole appreciated the fact that his aphorism applied to their business. And since it is frequently more difficult to think than to feel, it is often harder to maintain the sharp edge of comedy than of tragedy. The showman's toughest chore is to leave 'em laughing.

So it was natural that as Hollywood pursued the soul-saving laugh, from the days of slapstick through screwball comedy, bedroom farce, social satire and black humor, such deeply serious men as Frank Capra and Stanley Kubrick worked at this precarious task (even as some wildly funny individuals, John Huston for instance, paradoxically explored more somber subjects).

Among the most thoughtful practitioners of the difficult art was Howard Hawks, who described his technique in directing Cary Grant. "Grant is so easy to work with," Hawks once told LIFE movie critic Richard Schickel. "You do a scene and he says 'How's that?' And I say 'Pretty dull.' 'What's wrong with it?' And I say 'Well, the way you get angry.' We talk about one way and another way, and I might say 'I knew a fella that got so mad he'd whinny like a horse.' 'Oh,' he said. 'Let me do that.' And he did it and he was very funny."

William Wellman was less introspective about comedy and quite direct in his pursuit of it. LIFE reported that Wellman, known as Wild Bill, felt that "the way to get a cast into the spirit of a farce is to create the general atmosphere of a lunatic asylum." It delighted Wellman that Fredric March and Carole Lombard, the stars of his Ben Hecht satire *Nothing Sacred,* spent their lunch hours tearing around the studio in a fire truck (borrowed from the Los Angeles Fire Department for a

sequence in the film), its siren screaming. And he joined the two in shooting with air guns at the lights in the sound-stage roof. At the picture's end the cast gave him a straitjacket.

Charlie Chaplin was the rare genius who could demonstrate how close true comedy and true tragedy were to each other; and LIFE recognized and pursued this genius determinedly. When Chaplin made *The Great Dictator* in 1940, he closed the set and refused to release the pictures of himself as a mock Hitler (his character in the film was Adenoid Hynkel, Dictator of Tomania). Dick Pollard, LIFE's Hollywood correspondent, ordered to get a picture, paid a Chaplin film cutter $100 for a single frame and sent it to New York with a warning that it was copyrighted and that Chaplin could sue on publication. It was and he did, for a million dollars. But Chaplin settled out of court for a promise—which LIFE gave with barely concealed delight—of a 10-page story in the magazine.

There were some artists, of course, to whom plain, noncerebral comedy came naturally. Jimmy Durante bubbled with humor wherever he happened to be. But occasionally even the Schnoz could play it deadpan. LIFE ran the 1950 publicity picture at left with a deadpan performance of its own, derogating the kilted squirrel's pianistic technique and slovenly dress and saying of "the man partially visible in the background" only that he was "an actor appearing with the squirrel in a movie called *The Great Rupert."* Quite predictably, Durante wrote a Letter to the Editors: "Sir: Just bought a copy of LIFE in which you show the picture of an actor, a piano and a squirrel. I know the name of the squirrel. I know the name of the piano. Won't you please publish the name of the actor to relieve my curiosity as he has such a kind face."

Durante and friend do a duet in a picture LIFE used to comment on "the lengths to which certain creatures will go" for publicity. Pointing out that the squirrel "has absolutely no talent," and not mentioning Durante by name, LIFE added that the picture would not have run had it not offered "a fine view of a piano."

Deadpanned Chico Marx douses blonde Esther Muir with wallpaper paste in A Day at the Races (1937), thus offering a classic example of the brutal level to which slapstick comedy often descended.

In Safety Last (1923), Harold Lloyd swings on a clock. "A good deal of the picture hangs by its eyelashes along the face of a building," LIFE wrote. "The higher and more horrifying, the funnier it gets."

Charlie Chaplin could wring a laugh even out of a wet shoe—as he did in The Gold Rush (1925) by boiling his boot, eating the laces like spaghetti and consuming the leather, leaving the fishbone-like nails.

Reduced to one (luckily outsized) pair of pants in a scene from a potpourri of old films called The Golden Age of Comedy (1958), Laurel and Hardy handle their plight with typical insouciance.

Buster Keaton is right on target with an old standby of slapstick in Hollywood Cavalcade (1939). In admiration of Keaton's impeccable technique, LIFE called him "the Carl Hubbell of cinema pie-pitching."

In At the Circus (1939) Groucho Marx finds himself on top of a tent, where with the aid of trick photography he dances an inverted rumba with Eve Arden.

The shoving match between Fredric March and Carole Lombard in Nothing Sacred (1937) was described by LIFE as "the battle of the movie year."

Unaccustomed to such fanfare, a pregnant waitress (Marie Wilson) is dumfounded as James Cagney gestures and trumpets sound to herald the coming birth of her baby in Boy Meets Girl (1938).

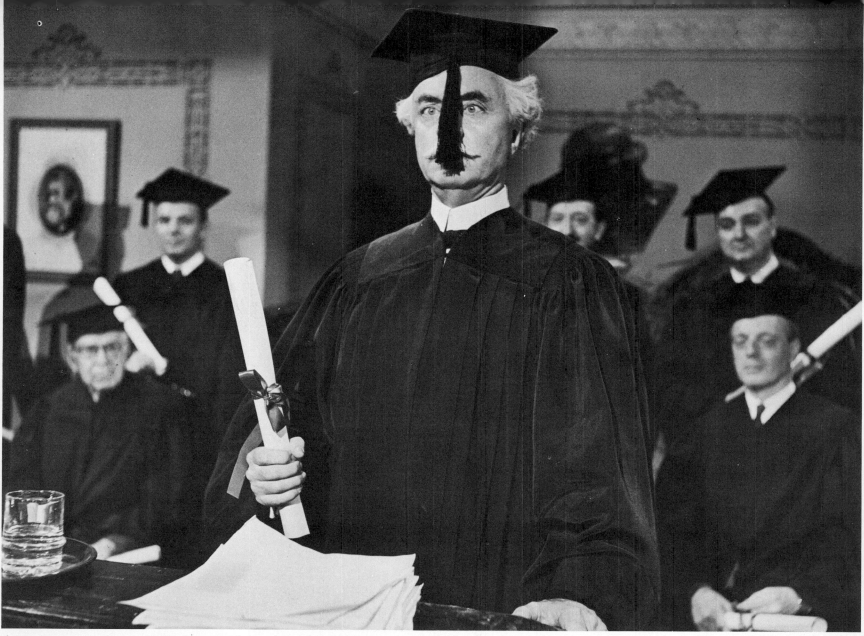

A tassel crosses up Senator Melvin Gassaway Ashton (played by William Powell) as he gets an honorary degree in animal husbandry in The Senator Was Indiscreet (1947).

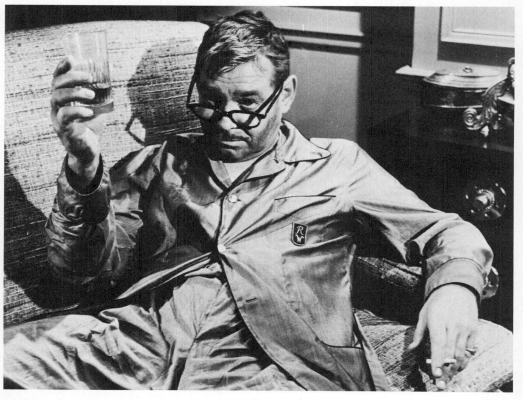

"Gable gassed is still glamorous," LIFE commented admiringly of the 58-year-old actor, who portrayed a middle-aged Casanova in But Not for Me (1959).

Cary Grant becomes a Wac during a wardrobe test for I Was a Male War Bride (1949), in which he masqueraded as a woman to be near his new bride.

Sozzled Julie Harris flops in her chair like a rag doll in I Am a Camera (1955). The general depravity and frank chatter in this comedy caused the Production Code Administration to withhold its seal.

Demonstrating that Hollywood's comediennes can be as zany as their male counterparts, Shirley MacLaine, the plucky "poule" of Irma La Douce (1963), swings from a chandelier in a raffish Paris café.

Doris Day emerges from an encounter with a car wash in Move Over, Darling (1963). The movie was a remake of Marilyn Monroe's uncompleted last film—but without Marilyn's publicized nude swimming scene.

In Adam's Rib (1949), Judy Holliday, a silly blonde with a pardonable desire to shoot her husband, prepares for the project by boning up on guns.

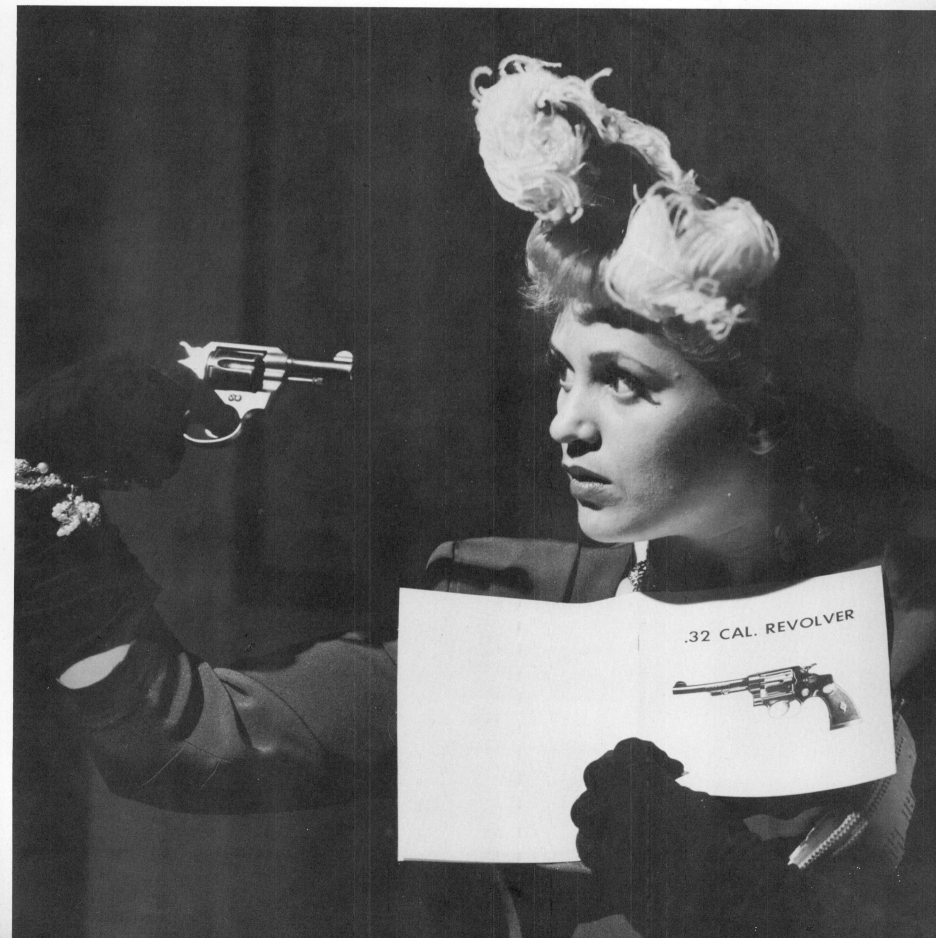

of the most successful attractions were low-budget films. In August 1938 LIFE's

MOVIE OF THE WEEK:

Love
Finds Andy Hardy

The current slump in box-office receipts has made even Hollywood producers wonder "What's wrong with the movies?" Condescending at last to examine their balance sheets, the movie moguls have discovered an interesting fact: many of the supercolossal, star-studded "specials" have been expensive flops, while certain low-budget pictures have quietly cleaned up. The most notable example is the series of *Judge Hardy* pictures made by M-G-M. Designed

for the family trade in small towns, they now as holdover attractions on Broadway.

The Hardy Family consists of four stock pl while other characters change from picture t ture. Judge Hardy presides over the local court town of Carvel, somewhere in the Middle Wes *You're Only Young Once* the Hardys vacation Catalina Island, where the daughter fell in love a lifeguard. In *Judge Hardy's Children*, the

1 The family: Lewis Stone as the Judge, Cecilia Parker as Marian, Fay Holden as Mrs. Hardy, Mickey Rooney as Andy.

2 Andy's regular girl, Polly (Ann Rutherford) is leaving. They kiss.

3 Andy pays $12 on a car, needs $8 more. A Jimmy, who is leaving town, offers to pay him

6 Betsy (Judy Garland) next enters Andy's life. He considers her, however, a mere child.

7 Mrs. Hardy is called away by her mother's illness. The Judge (and Augusta, the cook) read her letter.

8 Andy gets a friend to send Mrs. Hardy a over his short-wave radio. The Judge is

11 Just before Christmas, Andy receives a blow. Jimmy cannot pay the $8. Betsy sympathizes.

12 The Judge gives him $8 and a thrift talk, mentions that one day he will be dead. Andy is alarmed.

13 Jealous of Cynthia, Polly refuses to g big Christmas dance. He has to tak

33

Washington as head of a Federal commission
dy fell in love with the French Ambassador's
er.
ar as any one player is responsible for the
of the Judge Hardy pictures, it is Mickey
y. The latest and best of the series, *Love*
Andy Hardy, is almost entirely his. Young Mr.
y gives a portrait of an adolescent boy which
good as anything seen on the screen this year.

y is afraid other boys
steal his girl, Cynthia.

5 Andy's $8 job is to keep Cynthia (Lana Turner) dated up. She is very willing.

is well content with his bargain to keep
ia dated up, finds her "sensational."

10 She likes kissing best of all. That suits Andy.

tsy sings and
kes a great hit.

15 After leading the grand march (*right*) Andy drives Betsy home in his new car, elated.

Mickey Rooney and Judy Garland

The Epics

Hollywood was still very young when it realized that all of history and all of the classics of literature, old and new, were made to order for rich adaptation to the screen.

Epic: "Extending beyond the usual and ordinary, esp. in size or scope." Hollywood, which may have drained much of the meaning out of such words as "colossal," was, however, quite in agreement with Webster's definition of "epic." Such grandeur naturally appealed to moviemakers, and there were epics, or spectaculars, right from the beginning. A version of the Passion play was filmed, on the roof of New York's Grand Central Palace, as early as 1898. And 1907 saw a one-reel movie of *Ben-Hur.*

LIFE was not around for either of those early epics, of course; and it also missed D. W. Griffith's *Intolerance* (1916), whose cost ($2 million) some authorities hold to be the greatest of all time, relative to the contemporary price of potatoes. But early in its existence the magazine made up for lost time by running a "History of the World in Movie Stills," making the point—perhaps not without a touch of envy—that Hollywood was onto a good thing pictorially in re-creating history. In fact, LIFE suggested, Hollywood not only restaged history but also improved on it: "In actual history," said the article, "many of the great moments were undoubtedly dramatic flops—unimpressive, badly lighted and acted, cluttered with irrelevant detail."

History was indeed one of the movies' most profitable discoveries. Besides its authentic plots, it offered an inexhaustible supply of ready-made heroes, sinners, scalawags and lovers; and a bottomless trunk of fancy costumes, swords, tomahawks and crowns. The Bible alone was the repository of enough raw material for the whole industry. "Almost every personage in the Bible seems to have had a long-term contract with Hollywood," LIFE quipped—and at the same time published a number of the more memorable and dramatic Biblical scenes in a widescreen spread.

More worldly personages also served. Alexander Graham Bell, for example, had his historical identity stripped from him by Don Ameche, who portrayed him in *The Story of Alexander Graham Bell* (1939). Contemporary slang referred to the telephone as "the ameche," and World War II GIs made it almost standard nomenclature. It was said that some teachers had a difficult time persuading children that Ameche did *not* invent the thing.

If history had been made to order for the movies—an opinion widely held in Hollywood —literature was an even better provider. (In later years, of course, many books were written expressly for the films; few of them, however, would be mistaken for literature.)

One of the first assignments Peter Stackpole received upon being stationed in Hollywood was to set up base camp at the foot of 14,494-foot Mount Whitney, 230 miles northeast of Hollywood. RKO was using Whitney as a stand-in for a mountain in the Khyber Pass, for the filming of *Gunga Din.* Turning Kipling's poem about a regimental water boy into a spectacle, the studio built on the slopes a British army cantonment ($45,000), two complete villages ($75,000 apiece), a gold-domed temple ($85,000) and a city of 100 tents to house the cast, the crew and the 1,000 extras who were transported into the wild, along with 100 horses, eight camels, four elephants, 600 rifles, four cannons, two Gatling guns, 50,000 cartridges—and, no doubt, a pear tree.

Publishing a photograph by Stackpole of RKO's impressive exercise in verisimilitude *(left),* LIFE called *Gunga Din* the "greatest location picture in Hollywood history." Only for a time, however: its magnificence would be eclipsed from time to time thereafter. But that, of course, is motion picture history.

Kilted and pith-helmeted as Sepoy Lancers and alerted by the bugle of the regimental "bhisti," named Gunga Din, an army of extras charges up a Sierra slope in the 1939 spectacular based on Kipling's poem.

Great Spectacles

A surefire way to shout "Spectacle!" was to focus on real people and powerful events, and to throw in a Cast of Thousands. Then, of course, there was always the Bible.

The Crucifixion becomes an epic scene in The Robe (1953), the first movie filmed in CinemaScope and projected on a curved, elongated screen.

Russia's Sergei Eisenstein made a two-part classic of Ivan the Terrible (1945). Here the Czar watches his subjects coming to beg him not to abdicate.

Some actors became so intimately identified with the historic figures they portrayed tha

Ingrid Bergman as Joan of Arc (1948)

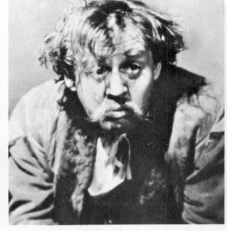

Charles Laughton as Rembrandt (1936)

Emil Jannings as Henry VIII (1921)

Walter Huston as Lincoln (1930)

Raymond Massey as Lincoln (1939)

Fredric March as Mark Twain (1944)

Marlon Brando and Jean Simmons as Napoleon and Désirée (1954)

Paul Muni as Emile Zola (1937)

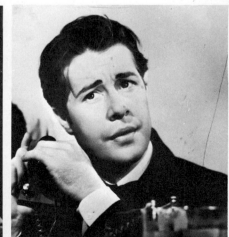

Don Ameche as Alexander G. Bell (1939)

After a time many a movie-goer had considerable difficulty distinguishing one from the other.

Norma Shearer as Marie Antoinette (1938)

Henry Wilcoxon and Claudette Colbert as Antony and Cleopatra (1934)

Bette Davis as Elizabeth I (1939)

Vivien Leigh as Lady Hamilton (1941)

Elizabeth Taylor as Cleopatra (1963)

José Ferrer as Toulouse-Lautrec (1952)

The Lure of Literature

*The literary country claimed by Hollywood was boundless.
It stretched from Shakespeare's England to Twain's
Missouri and points east and west—including Shangri-La.*

The studios—and the editors—knew that the stories were surefire and the audience presold whenever Hollywood turned for its plots to properties that had already won widespread popular acceptance: the classics of literature or books that had recently climbed high on the sales charts. Audiences and readers alike responded strongly whenever familiar print was transferred to Celluloid.

Given this very practical advantage, producers bought further commercial insurance with lavish productions and high-powered casting. These visual ingredients made such films that much more attractive as fodder for LIFE's pages—but did not inhibit the magazine's reviews from occasionally labeling a multimillion-dollar dud as precisely that.

Scheming to "catch the English crown" for himself, Sir Laurence Olivier in Richard III (1956) turns his back on the high pomp of his brother's coronation.

◀ Orson Welles in the title role of Macbeth (1948) concludes a contract with hired killers. Welles's Scottish accent so blurred his performance that LIFE commented he "doth foully slaughter Shakespeare."

In a moving scene from Marjorie Kinnan Rawlings' novel The Yearling (1946), Claude Jarman Jr., as Jody Baxter, a boy who hopes vainly to raise a pet deer to maturity, gives the animal a tender rubdown.

Young Pip (Anthony Wager) listens as a conspiratorial Miss Havisham (Martita Hunt) urges him to fall in love with an aristocratic girl in Dickens' study of class-consciousness, Great Expectations (1947).

In the prized title role of Twain's The Adventures of Tom Sawyer, Tommy Kelly, plucked from obscurity (and soon to return there), saunters along a dusty Missouri road.

◄ *His craggy face creased in desperate determination, Spencer Tracy is an epic by himself as the fisherman who battles a giant marlin in the film adaptation of Hemingway's The Old Man and the Sea (1958).*

Zombie-like, Omar Sharif stumbles in misery through a Siberian blizzard in Dr. Zhivago (1965), an $11-million treatment of Pasternak's novel that LIFE said was "worth all the work and money—and almost every moment of its 197-minute running time."

Vivien Leigh takes Anna Karenina's famous last walk on the railroad tracks in the 1948 version of the Tolstoy novel. Anna Karenina was filmed at least three other times, twice with Garbo as the star.

Foul weather thwarts Merle Oberon's search for Heathcliff in Wuthering Heights (1939), which LIFE said captured "the high passions and the dour moods" of Emily Brontë's melancholy English classic.

As deranged by his obsession with the white whale as the whale is maddened by the harpoons, Ahab (Gregory Peck) goes to the bottom with his quarry in the climactic scene from Moby Dick (1956).

Kicking up clouds of bottom sand, divers in outfits designed to look Victorian and yet work with modern efficiency stride the ocean floor in Disney's 1954 filming of Jules Verne's 1869 classic, 20,000 Leagues Under the Sea. The cover picture was made by Peter Stackpole, a crack underwater photographer.

To all intents and purposes, the five men who ran the five major studios during the '30s controlled the movies. As long as the bottom line appeared in rich black, the Eastern financiers kept their hands off. Tyrants these Hollywood tycoons were, but they also responded with gut respect to the talent that delivered theater audiences.

The Studio

During the 1930s the movies became a kind of religion for the masses and Hollywood was a cathedral town. In the latter years of the decade, the annual procession of the faithful through the box-office turnstiles amounted to twice the population of the world. The places of worship, Hollywood's major studios, were top-sacred sanctums where only the anointed—employees or specially invited guests—might enter; the ticket-buying public could only gaze in awe at the studio walls and speculate on the wondrous goings-on within. (Years later, in the early 1960s, studio boss Lew Wasserman began cashing in on this continuing curiosity by providing organized guided tours of the new Universal City studio.)

In a 1939 show, *Set to Music,* Bea Lillie memorialized the devotion of fans of the day with Noel Coward's lyrics for *Mad About the Boy.* Assuming the accent of a cockney maid, she sang: "Every Wednesday afternoon I get a little time off from three to eleven,/Then I go to the Picture House/And taste a little of my particular heaven."

There were millions of particular heavens around the world in the '30s, and the studio moguls—who tended to behave as if they were indeed deities—took particular pains to keep it that way. Even though the private behavior of some stars might be deplorable, their public images were those of a band of angels—and anyone who said otherwise was subject to excommunication. In 1941, when Budd Schulberg dared to expose Hollywood's backstage squalor in his classic novel *What Makes Sammy Run?* the reaction was shocked disbelief; how could a prince of the blood, himself the native son of one of the old-line movie chiefs, commit such a heresy? In a LIFE article, Schulberg reported the rage of L. B. Mayer, lord of M-G-M, when he met Budd's father, B. P. Schulberg, once head of Paramount:

"He took B. P. aside and his voice trembled with emotion. 'How could you let him do it?'

" 'Do what?'

" 'Write that horrible book—it's a disgrace to The Industry—subversive, disloyal. . . . Blacklisting is too good for him. I don't think you take this seriously enough, B. P. He should be *deported!*' "

If an incipient star's real features and personality did not measure up to the standard mold, the studio was quite capable of and ever ready to improve on nature—often to the point where the ambitious young arrival became unrecognizable. Hair was recolored and restyled, bosoms were lifted or enlarged, shoulders padded, noses reshaped, freckles bleached out, eyebrows and lips redrawn, names changed, Bronx or Southern accents corrected. From pruning back

Rita Hayworth's hairline to restructuring Clark Gable's teeth to changing Frances Gumm's name to Judy Garland, the studio hierarchy felt free to manufacture its production-line fair ladies and gentlemen. A Barbra Streisand or a Dustin Hoffman would have made it in the old Hollywood only after drastic renovations.

Hollywood was, after all, a town that flourished on the word yes. Although they derived their authority from the main business offices back in New York (a three-day train trip from Hollywood during the '30s), the studio chiefs held absolute sway over their own lots—as long as the cash receipts poured in. They dictated how many pictures would be made each year, who would direct and act in them, how much money and time would be expended on each film, and which players would be promoted to stardom or doomed to oblivion. They were, in too many instances, unlettered vulgarians or formula-bound entrepreneurs—men who wanted to tack happy endings onto classic tragedies, or who spoke in strange tongues ("I'll tell you in two words . . ." Sam Goldwyn once said, ". . . im-possible!"), and who took for granted the supine loyalty of everyone employed by, or associated with, the studio. Harry Cohn, the tyrant of Columbia Pictures, went so far as to bug the dressing rooms of his stars so he could tune in on their indiscretions and disloyalties. Yet stories about such goings on rarely appeared in print; and those were payoffs to reporters on the Hollywood beat who played ball by perpetuating the plastic façade.

While several minor studios ground out minor films (Republic, for example), and a few talented independent producers like Selznick and Goldwyn and Disney flourished on their own, the real power and glory that was Hollywood was concentrated in just five studios, which were held in thrall by their bosses: at M-G-M, Mayer (with, for a time, Irving Thalberg); at Warner Brothers, Jack Warner; at Paramount, Schulberg; at 20th Century-Fox, Darryl Zanuck; and at Columbia, Cohn. These five studios *were* the film industry, and the men who ran them decided what the audiences of the world would see. But while they served up a considerable portion of garbage and wasted the talents of too many accomplished actors, writers and directors, they also delivered up feasts to the popular taste: moving dramas, rollicking comedies and eye-filling spectacles that stood as landmarks in the development of motion pictures as an original American art form.

The silhouetted film crew on the cover of LIFE's 1963 double year-end issue, "The Movies," could have been working on any Hollywood back lot, but was actually shooting a film in Tokyo's Toho Studio.

LIFE

TWO-IN-ONE ISSUE **35** CENTS

The Moviemakers

*Sometimes the public at large could only dimly perceive
their gifts, but the legendary directors and producers
left their distinctive signatures on every film they made.*

Connoisseurs of the art of films do not need credits flashed on the screen to identify the work of a master director; they can spot a Hitchcock, a Bergman or a Fellini as quickly as an art curator can recognize a Rembrandt, a Goya or a Picasso. It was not always so: in the years between Hollywood's emergence as a mighty industry and the era of great change after World War II, the majority of directors and producers marched to the tune of the studio bosses. In his 1963 memoir in LIFE, novelist and screenwriter Budd Schulberg reminisced about Harry Cohn, the notoriously terrible-tempered czar of Columbia studios: "If you were a director, you didn't talk back to Harry's gestapo system. Assistant directors were ordered to call in from the set to inform the boss how many takes his shackled maestro had in the can by 10 a.m." The effect was to encourage an avalanche of chaff. The public nevertheless ate it all up: no matter what was playing at the Roxy, going there each week was almost obligatory, little less so than going to church on Sunday.

There were, of course, first-rate films of memorable, even enduring excellence that managed to surmount the creative obstacles But while the players who starred in them were unstintingly worshipped, who among the audiences that cheered Bette Davis in *Of Human Bondage* and Clark Gable in *Gone With the Wind* remembered that John Cromwell and Victor Fleming directed them? Was there ever a Fred Zinnemann Fan Club? Sadly, the men who made the cast assignments, edited the scenarios, and wheedled and bullied the players were in the main anonymous heroes.

In the beginning when the movies first got out of their nickelodeon knickers into 12-reel maturity, the director—with his pith helmet and megaphone—was an identifiable charac-

ter, often more prominent than the stars themselves. Everybody knew that D. W. Griffith directed *Birth of a Nation*. Erich von Stroheim and Charlie Chaplin were noted directors as well as actors. Then, in 1922, Irving Thalberg, the efficient young general manager of Universal studios, fired Stroheim in the midst of a film production for his extravagant spending. It was the first time a studio head had dared impose his will on a powerful director and it marked the beginning of the long years of bondage to the bosses.

Nevertheless, some directorial giants managed to develop personal hallmarks. Acres of Roman legionnaires or Claudette Colbert in a bath of asses' milk could only mean C. B. De Mille. And when, in *Ninotchka,* audiences saw Garbo as a grimly unfeminine Soviet comrade looking wistfully at a frivolous little hat in a Paris shop window, they recognized the "Lubitsch touch." Alfred Hitchcock was the acknowledged technical master of film making. His genius came through clearly in his stunning montages and sudden cuts, and he added a whimsical, personal colophon to each film—a cameo appearance of the portly maestro himself.

With the passing of the big-studio era, directors and independent producers came into their own. What had started as an exclusively American enterprise became multinational, with Italian, French, English, Swedish and Japanese directors showing audiences what could be accomplished with a camera and inspiration. It was a new ball game, in which the director got the top billing, and cults, if not fan clubs, gathered around him. As Hitchcock told LIFE's Robert Coughlan in 1963: "Naturally, there has to be a story, but it is not the content of the story that counts nearly so much as the content of the director."

Frank Capra, a gardener before he became one of filmdom's top directors, looks over some of the 62 miles of film he shot for You Can't Take It With You (1938) before pruning it back to a workable length.

The Director's Chair

Many of the faces behind the camera were to become as familiar as those on the screen, and not a few of them demonstrated more genuine star quality than their stars.

On location with Lolita (1962), director Stanley Kubrick looks worried—as well he might, considering the problem of reconciling the Motion Picture Production Code and Vladimir Nabokov's story of a middle-aged man's lust for a 12-year-old nymphet.

George Stevens peers through a view finder at a scene from The Diary of Anne Frank (1959). LIFE photographer Ralph Crane focused on the director's sunglasses and caught this reflection.

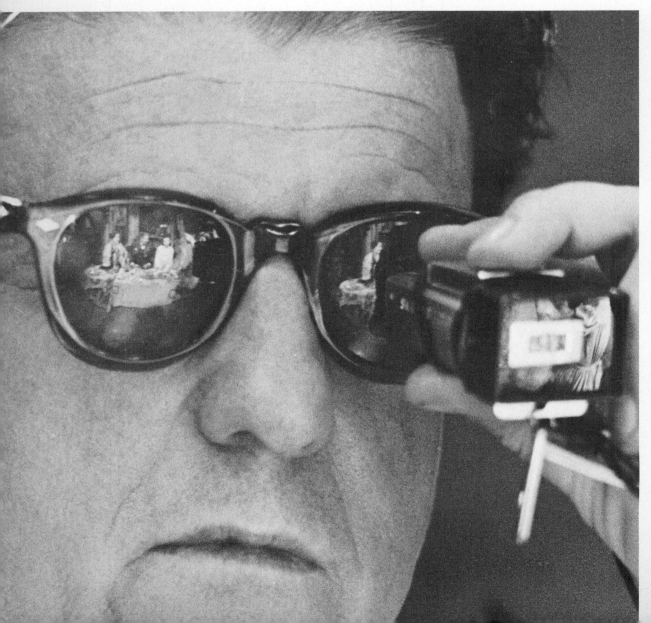

Wearing the jodhpurs and boots that were his trademark, Cecil B. De Mille waves commands to Moses and the Israelites as they emerge from the Red Sea in The Ten Commandments (1956). It was his second version of the epic; he did the first in 1923.

Sizing up the scene on Pennsylvania Avenue, Otto Preminger prepares to shoot a take of his Washington blockbuster, Advise and Consent (1961), while Henry Fonda and Charles Laughton stand by.

Comedian-turned-director Mike Nichols assumes a commanding stance before his all-star cast while filming Joseph Heller's Catch 22 (1970). At left, foreground: star Alan Arkin as Captain Yossarian.

On location, director John Huston watches the action in his faithful translation of Stephen Crane's Civil War classic The Red Badge of Courage (1951).

Alfred Hitchcock, the roly-poly master of horror films, poses for a LIFE cover with three affable avian aggressors from his gruesome movie The Birds (1963).

Shirley MacLaine "strangles" herself with the sleeves of director Billy Wilder's sweater in a moment of horseplay on the set of The Apartment (1960). "There's a limit to togetherness," Wilder said, and switched to sleeveless sweaters.

On a 1914 set, the pioneer director of silent films, D. W. Griffith, explains a suicide scene to his cameraman and to matinee idol Henry B. Walthall.

With centurions standing by (background), pipe-smoking Joseph Mankiewicz discusses with Martin Landau (left) and Rex Harrison, battle plans for final scenes in Cleopatra (1963), the $40-million extravaganza.

Charlie Chaplin tells a windblown Marlon Brando how to act seasick for a storm-tossed sequence in *The Countess From Hong Kong* (1967), which Chaplin both wrote and directed. He also wrote in a walk-on part for himself as a ship's steward.

Preston Sturges, from his customary tutorial position before the camera, instructs Harold Lloyd and Frances Ramsden in *The Sin of Harold Diddlebock* (1947), an erratic comedy about a bookkeeper turned gambler that Sturges produced with Howard Hughes.

While filming *Angel* (1937), an amused Dietrich bends to the Ernst Lubitsch touch as he demonstrates to Herbert Marshall how not to hug a lady.

A natatorial Garbo hangs on every word of George Cukor's instructions for a poolside sequence in *Two-Faced Woman* (1941), the last film she ever made.

The Foreign Touch

After World War II, stunning films came out of France, Italy, Scandinavia and Japan. Directed by philosophers of the cinematic art, they changed moviemaking forever.

Japan's finest director, Akira Kurosawa, stands before a blowup of actor Toshiro Mifune in Seven Samurai (1954), a medieval spectacle that John Sturges redid as a Western, The Magnificent Seven (1960).

On the set of The Clowns (1971), Federico Fellini dons make-up to illustrate what he called the "half magic, half slaughterhouse" nature of a circus.

Making Blow-Up (1966), his first film in English, Michelangelo Antonioni halts production to ask his dialogue director if the words sound authentic. The movie's star, David Hemmings, waits at left.

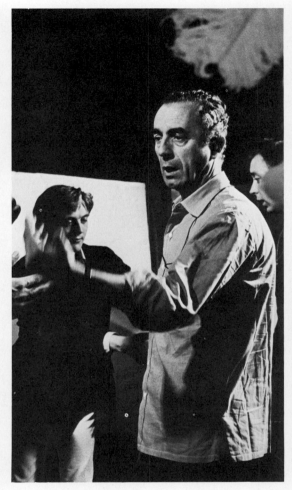

Ingmar Bergman, the Swedish master director who excited filmdom and took dozens of prizes for his often baffling movies, walks across the set of The Devil's Eye (1961), a story set in hell.

Julie Christie, star of Fahrenheit 451 (1966), lunches with Francois Truffaut; she called him "a truly great director, the kind of man you want to love."

The Producers

In the make-believe world of movies, the buck stopped —and began—with the producers, all-powerful men who controlled everything from bankrolling to distribution.

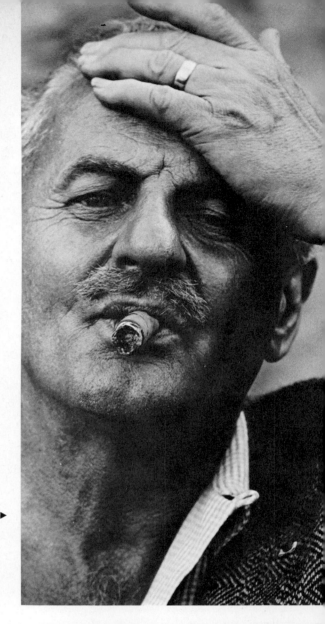

Tough Harry Cohn ran Columbia studios from 1920 to 1958 like a feudal demesne. Of movie production, he said: "It's not a business—it's a racket."

As commander in chief of 20th Century-Fox, anguished ▶ Darryl Zanuck landed 1,600 troops on Omaha Beach, re-creating the Normandy invasion in The Longest Day (1962) for some $10 million.

One of the original "fur, glove and junk merchants" who built the industry, Sam Goldwyn was famous for solecisms ("Include me out"), but made quality movies and became dean of Hollywood moguls.

Framed in a "bug-eye" lens used with his widescreen Todd-AO cameras, Mike Todd—with his inevitable cigar —oversees the filming of Oklahoma! (1955).

◄ David O. Selznick, producer of Gone With the Wind (1939), was shot by LIFE against an Alpine-warfare photomural from A Farewell to Arms (1957).

Making The Outlaw (1943), the Western that introduced Jane Russell, Howard Hughes drove cast and crew hard, but overshot his budget by $3,250,000.

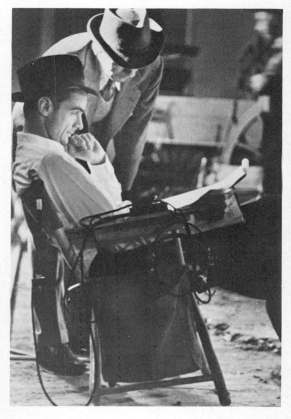

203

At its peak M-G-M was the biggest and the richest studio in the world with a repertory

Louis B. Mayer is surrounded by his top talent in a 1943 command muster set up for LIFE. From left, first row: James Stewart, Margaret Sullavan, Lucille Ball, Hedy Lamarr, Katharine Hepburn, Mayer, Greer Garson, Irene Dunne, Susan Peters, Ginny Simms, Lionel Barrymore. Second row: Harry James, Brian Donlevy, Red Skelton, Mickey Rooney, William Powell, Wallace Beery, Spencer Tracy, Walter Pidgeon, Robert Taylor, Pierre Au- mont, Lewis Stone, Gene Kelly, Jackie Jenkins. Third row: Tommy Dorsey, George Murphy, Jean Rogers, James Craig, Donna Reed, Van Johnson, Fay Bainter, Marsha Hunt, Ruth Hussey, Marjorie Main, Robert

company of contract players that was unmatched. And when the big boss said, "Sit!"...

Benchley. Fourth row: Dame May Whitty, Reginald Owen, Keenan Wynn, Diana Lewis, Marilyn Maxwell, Esther Williams, Ann Richards, Martha Linden, Lee Bowman, Richard Carlson, Mary Astor. Fifth row: Blanche Ring, Sara Haden, Fay Holden, Bert Lahr, Frances Gifford, June Allyson, Richard Whorf. Frances Rafferty, Spring Byington, Connie Gilchrist, Gladys Cooper. Sixth row: Ben Blue, Chill Wills, Keye Luke, Barry Nelson, Desi Arnaz, Henry O'Neill, Bob Crosby, Rags Ragland. Among the distinguished absentees: Judy Garland, Charles Laughton, Clark Gable, Robert Montgomery, Lana Turner, Laraine Day, Robert Young, Ann Sothern.

The Production Line

Manufacturing dreams into films grew into a huge and complex industry. Its raw materials were human ingenuity and patience; its tools, technology and tricks of the eye.

In Hollywood's uncomplicated early youth, film making was not much more difficult than taking snapshots with a Brownie. But as the business burgeoned from a cottage industry amid the California orange groves into an industrial colossus and a universal habit, the process of movie production became ever more complicated and expensive. Where an oldtime moviemaker needed only a sunny day and a corporal's guard of assistants, the new breed demanded battalions of technicians to get their illusions on film. After Al Jolson yelled for his "Mammy" through the tinny voice of Vitaphone in 1927 and Hollywood came indoors to the cavernous sound stages, legions of new specialists—from master mixers to voice coaches—swarmed to the studios. After sound came Technicolor and then CinemaScope and Todd AO and every kind of wonder, each new process requiring new expertise.

Not uniquely, the trade unions helped to swell the long ranks of production crews by featherbedding; and many producers, directors and stars inflated their egos by demanding, and getting, personal entourages. A self-respecting superstar could not hold her head up without a maid, a hairdresser, a make-up man, a couple of wardrobe women and perhaps a manicurist hovering around her like drones around a queen bee. In this atmosphere there was also constant competition to reach the pinnacle of panache. During the filming of *Marie Antoinette* (1938), producer Hunt Stromberg strove to get into the act by resorting to a silent-era ploy. He hired musicians to play, not for the sound track, but for the cast between scenes, in order to sustain a "proper mood."

It also fell to the legions of men and women laboring off-camera to hide the esthetic flicker in the magic lantern. When layers of make-up could no longer disguise the ravages of time in close-ups of an aging generation of glamor girls, cinematographers learned to smear Vaseline on the camera lens, or to photograph through gauze; and —*voilà!* the image became a little blurry, perhaps, but there was nary a crowsfoot to be seen. For the same no-expense-spared production of *Marie Antoinette,* 115 hair stylists were mustered into service to make sure that not one hair was out of place in the coiffures of Norma Shearer and the ladies of the French Court.

During those supercolossal days, all roads led to the movie set. The scenario for *Going Hollywood* (1933) called for a scene in Grand Central Terminal and it never occurred to M-G-M to put the troupe on a train for New York to shoot the real thing. Studio carpenters hammered out a facsimile on the studio lot so realistic that the most spavined commuter, viewing the film, never doubted that it was really Grand Central.

Later, with the postwar encroachments of TV and foreign films, with the decline and fall of box-office grosses and the public's refusal to accept million-dollar mediocrity, with the introduction of lighter, more portable cameras, the producers had hard second thoughts about their business and decided to go outdoors again, on location, to exotic climes where labor was cheaper and the scenery authentic. When Budd Schulberg revisited his old hometown on a LIFE assignment in 1963, he found that the best and brightest stars and directors were off in Yugoslavia, or Argentina, or Kenya, or Spain, and the studios were, for them, mere mail drops. "Where *was* Hollywood?," Schulberg asked. "How could I write about it? I couldn't even find it."

Bathed in spotlights, gowned in satin, fussed over by a wardrobe mistress and a hairdresser, Natalie Wood, every pampered inch the star, waits to face the camera in Sex and the Single Girl (1964).

Supernumeraries required by technology or by industry politics swelled the ranks of off-camera assistants—and the cost of moviemaking—enormously. (John Huston, preparing to film *The Night of the Iguana* (1964) in Mexico, was chagrined to learn that he would have to add a member of the Mexican S.P.C.A. to his payroll, to look after the iguanas.) On the set for *The Razor's Edge* (1946) at right, photographed for LIFE by Ralph Crane, Tyrone Power, in a tender moment, kisses Gene Tierney, unobserved save by director Edmund Goulding and 50 assorted technicians, whose functions are listed below, plus 30 others who do not appear in the picture. The scene was shot in three days, ran four minutes, 25 seconds in the finished film, and cost $70,714—surely one of the costliest kisses ever.

1 Director Goulding	27 Greenery Man
2 Gaffer (electrician)	28 Special-Effects Man
3 Photography Director	29 Grip
4 Assistant Cameraman	30 Sound-Boom Man
5 Assistant Cameraman	31 Grip
6 Camera Operator	32 Still Photographer
7 Crane Operator	33 Assistant Prop Man
8 Key Grip (Head Stagehand)	34 Prop Man
9 Best Boy (Assistant Gaffer)	35 Sound-Cable Man
	36 Assistant Sound Engineer
10 Grip	37 Stand-in for Power
11 Crane Operator	38 Stand-in for Tierney
12 Crane Steerer	39 Follow-up Man (Production Coordinator)
13 Dialogue Assistant	
14 Second Assistant Director	40 Mixer (Sound Engineer)
15 Fireman	41 Electrician
16 Crane Steerer	42 Electrician
17 Technical Advisor	43 Electrician
18 Painter	44 Assistant Prop Man
19 Script Clerk	45 Make-up Man
20 Electrician	46 Make-up Man
21 Grip	47 Hairdresser
22 Assistant Director	48 Wardrobe Girl
23 Unit Production Manager	49 Wardrobe Man
	50 Electrician
24 Fixture Man	51 Electrician
25 Contact Man	52 Hero Power
26 Second Assistant Director	53 Heroine Tierney

His solid-gold buss finally completed, Tyrone Power studies the script in the guaranteed isolation (except for LIFE's photographer) of a steam cabinet.

The children of Israel are not heading for the Promised Land pursued by the Egyptians, but their movie counterparts from The Ten Commandments (1956) are making a sunset exodus for home after a day's shooting. Cecil B. DeMille assembled a cast of more than 7,000 to reenact the Old Testament story.

In rehearsal for a big battle scene from *Spartacus* (1960), director Stanley Kubrick was inspired to number the "corpses" so he could call out directions by digits rather than just shout "You there!"

In *Lawrence of Arabia* (1962), Peter O'Toole practices crawling to the rescue of a guide trapped in quicksand, while two production crewmen stand by to sweep away the dry-run tracks before actual filming.

Perched on a boom over the Argentine pampas, J. Lee Thompson, at left, directs 6,000 gauchos masquerading as Russian cossacks and Polish cavalry in flaming battle for Taras Bulba (1962). The film, based on Gogol's novel about a hot-blooded father and his rebellious son, starred Yul Brynner and Tony Curtis.

Off Guard on Location

As film producers took to the road, in search of authentic locales and substitutes for expensive sets, performers found themselves doing odd things under odd conditions.

Gina Lollobrigida hula-hoops it up between takes of Solomon and Sheba (1959) on location in Spain. Yul Brynner played king to her sinuous queen.

On the set of Night of the Iguana (1964), in a hamlet on Mexico's Pacific coast, Richard Burton and Deborah Kerr break into an impromptu music-hall turn.

Melina Mercouri dazzles leading man Tony Perkins on the isle of Hydra while filming Phaedra (1962), a modern version of an ancient Greek tragedy.

Resting his football-fragile legs, Joe Namath is calm about his debut as a leading man in C. C. and Company (1970), a motorcycle saga filmed partly in the desert out West.

Between scenes of Picnic (1956), on location in Kansas, Susan Strasberg spoons ice cream for Kim Novak to ensure that her dress will not get spotted.

Pamela Franklin, all 78 pounds of her, cuddles up to a drowsy Zamba, 550-pound star of The Lion (1962), a Born Free-style jungle drama made in Kenya.

215

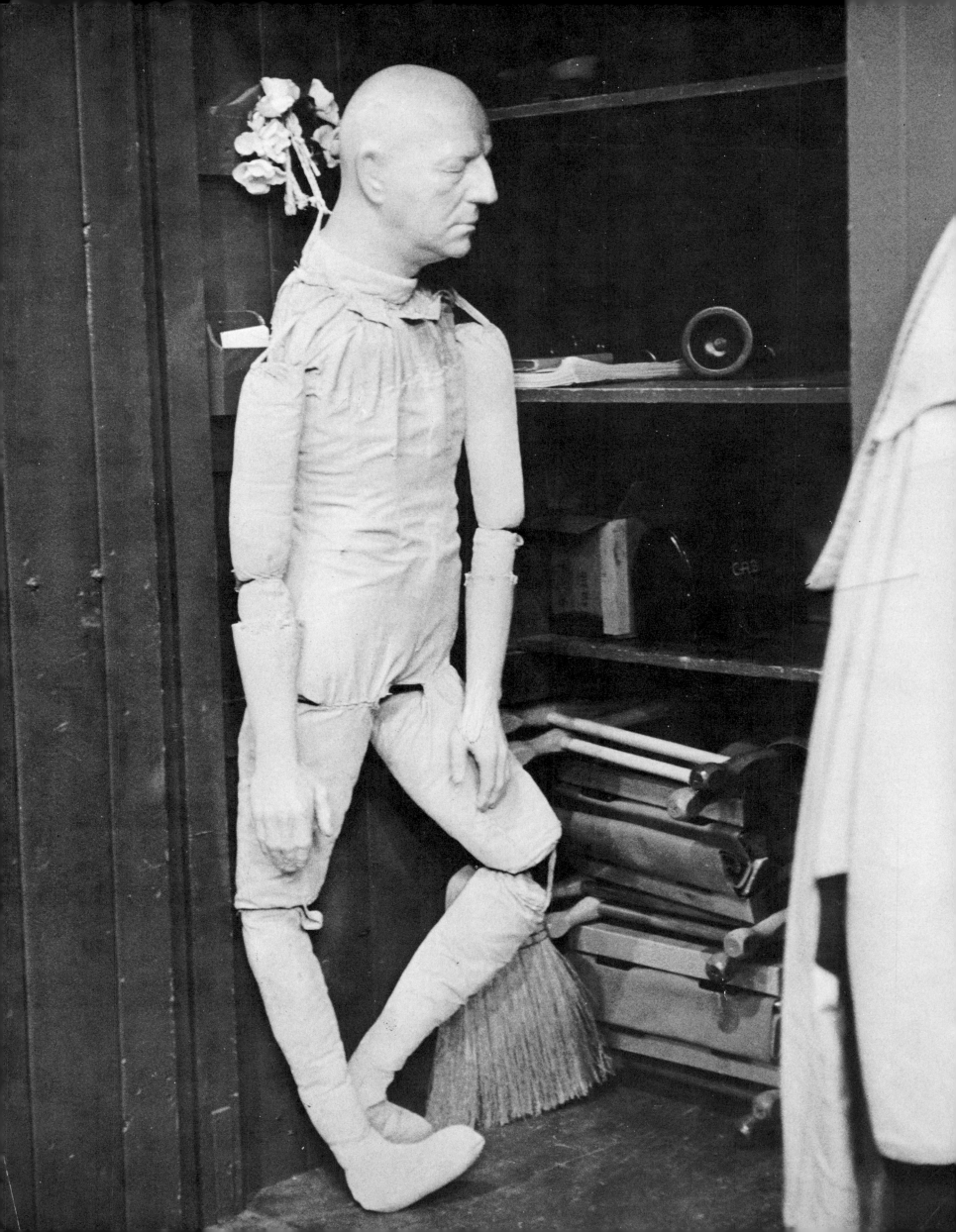

Grand Illusions

*The studios practiced to deceive upon the silver screen,
and the fans went along with the gag willingly—as
long as all the make-believe was absolutely believable.*

Everybody—at least, practically everybody—knew that much of what occurred on the screen was not what it appeared to be, from bustlines to train wrecks. Fakery added extra curves to sex godesses, made possible the acrobatic derring-do of swashbuckling heroes, and arrogantly duplicated earth-shaking acts of God.

Of *course* things weren't what they seemed. But what *were* they? LIFE found out. It poked around the studio lots, ferreting out the trickery, and showed how it was done. It didn't hurt the movie business—it's fun to be fooled, everyone said—and it served to introduce the readers to an elite band of artists who with make-up, special effects and stunts conjured up the magic on the screen.

A perennial assignment for LIFE photographers was a call upon one of the Westmores, the royal family of make-up. By 1945 the Westmore brothers—Wally, Bud, Perc (pronounced *purse),* Frank and Ernest had doctored the looks of more than 90 per cent of the stars and had trained three-quarters of the industry's make-up crews. Among their achievements were Bud's creation of the scaly tail that Ann Blyth splashed sportively in *Mr. Peabody and the Mermaid* (1948), and Wally's man-to-monster metamorphosis of Fredric March in *Dr. Jekyll and Mr. Hyde* (1932), in which March won an Oscar.

Most movie make-up work simply made the stars look the way the public wanted them to look, which meant such chores as narrowing the bridge of Claudette Colbert's nose, obliterating Shirley MacLaine's freckles, and not removing but emphasizing the lines that gave Humphrey Bogart's face that lived-in look. Some films, however, called for a maximum effort by studio disguise artists. For *Planet of the Apes* (1968), John Chambers, a mas-

ter technician who had made cosmetic and prosthetic replacement parts for disfigured servicemen, marshaled what was probably the largest make-up crew ever, 78 artists, to create a mini-civilization of orangutans, chimps and gorillas. That time it was the make-up man who won the Oscar.

While the make-up men quietly went about their work, the studio lot hummed with the sometimes wild goings on of the special-effects crews. Visiting Universal in 1963, LIFE found studio gardeners mowing lawns in front of tranquil homes with false fronts, and stuffed lions riding off to fake jungles in dollies. The special-effects master was George Pal. A Hungarian-born puppeteer, Pal had a genius for animation and miniaturization that was equally at home creating the fairy-tale world of *Tom Thumb* (1958), or the cataclysms of *When Worlds Collide* (1951).

Less illusory were the feats of the stunt men and stunt women who doubled for the stars in dangerous scenes. These specialists actually crashed the planes, collided the autos, drove the chariots and fell off an extraordinary number of horses. In the early days the risk was considerable. Studio records show that from 1925 to 1930 stunt men suffered thousands of injuries and more than 50 were killed.

The man who ended the era of carnage was one of the greatest stunters of all, Yakima Canutt, a former rodeo champion. Yak devised techniques for executing horse-and-rider falls (of which he himself took hundreds) with relative safety for both the stunter and the horse, and used them in later years as an action director. Despite the constant clashing of 5,000 extras and thousands of horses and camels in the battle sequences he filmed for *Khartoum* (1966), the scenes were so meticulously planned that there was not a single injury.

The rag-doll likeness of Louis Calhern that stood in for the fallen leader in Julius Caesar (1953) hangs limply on the wall of the studio property room. Calhern refused to let it take his place while the cameras were turning. After one take, he rose from the dead and said, "Let's do that again—I wasn't very good."

The Art of Make-up

Hollywood's Pygmalions made beauty out of dross (and vice versa), aged the young (also vice versa) and worked magic, good and bad, on beloved faces and bodies.

The magical changes wrought by the movie make-up men were natural fodder for LIFE's photographers. They regularly dropped by to watch the wizardry in what was known around the studios as the "bags and sags" department. In that brightly lighted enclave, man devolved into wild beast, youth leaped into Methuselah-like old age, Occidental turned Oriental. Technicians irreverently but deftly performed cosmetic surgery on moviedom's most beloved physiognomies and physiques.

The art of movie make-up had begun, in the early silent days, with conventional wigs, creams, powders and rouges; but technology had inevitably intervened and by the 1950s the eyebrow-pencilers had become a school of pseudo-anatomists, transforming their subjects by resorting to foam upholstery, latex masks, contact lenses and other contraptions and devices.

With these materials technicians scored such spectacular triumphs as making centenarians of Dustin Hoffman in *Little Big Man* and Agnes Moorehead in *The Lost Moment,* and transforming Homo sapiens into another kind of primate for *Planet of the Apes.*

 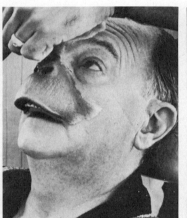 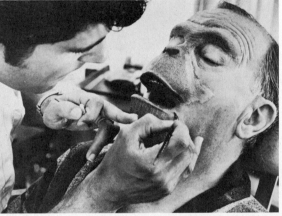

Step by step, technicians convert the features of Shakespearean actor Maurice Evans into what LIFE called "the wily-looking orangutan under the umbrella" for Planet of the Apes (1968). Evans was pleased to discover that he could manipulate his facial muscles and even sweat through the foam-rubber mask.

Youthful Dustin Hoffman, looking like himself (at left) in The Graduate (1967), became a 121-year-old survivor (below) of Custer's Last Stand in Little Big Man (1970). The 14-piece mask creating the hoary visage took five hours to apply. Said Hoffman to LIFE: "I defy anyone to put on that make-up and not feel old."

Swarthy make-up, chin whiskers and a putty nose make Anthony Quinn look as Arabian as his stallion for his sheikly role in Lawrence of Arabia (1962). In the insert, looking more like his real Mexican-Irish self, is Quinn as Henry II in the Broadway hit Becket.

Tony Randall pulls off one face before donning another in Seven Faces of Dr. Lao (1964), a whimsical Western in which he played a Chinese quick-change artist. Make-up men began by shearing his pate—his eyebrows too—before rendering him unrecognizable as the inscrutable Dr. Lao (insets).

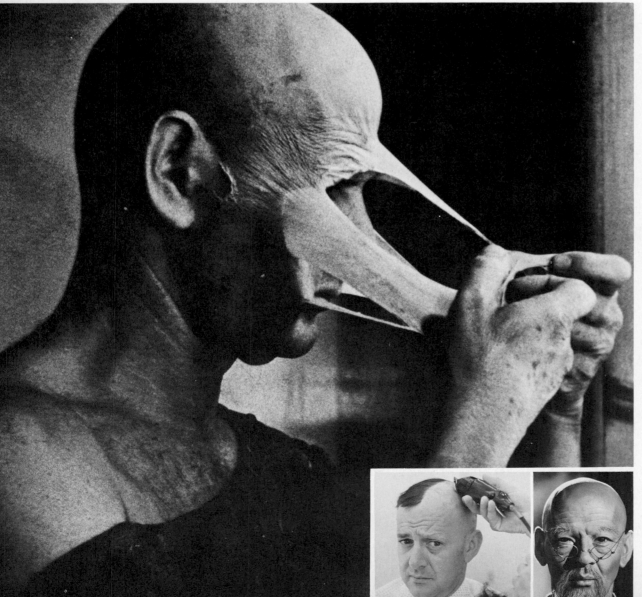

Shirley MacLaine, reflecting the Japanese she played in My Geisha (1962), appeared twice on one cover. Brown contact lenses, a wig and deft use of the make-up brush orientalized the blue-eyed redhead.

For lovely Agnes Moorehead (inset) the metamorphosis into a 110-year-old widow in The Lost Moment (1947) was a grueling ordeal. Artists glued a rubber mask to her face, then applied an overlay of wrinkles and wens. Agnes found the whole experience pretty painful. But the effect was impressively realistic.

LIFE's Alfred Eisenstaedt, always inventive, queried the make-up artist Wally Westmore

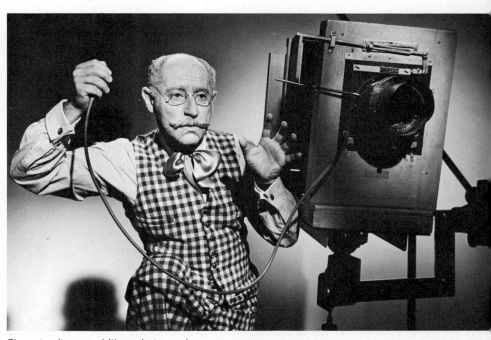

Eisenstaedt as an oldtime photographer

The real Eisie on the job, in coveralls and with his camera at the ready

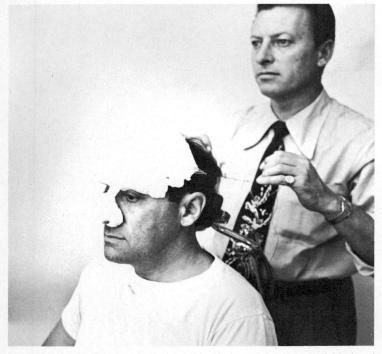

Westmore's first step in creating evil Mr. Hyde: a fake nose and forehead

Groucho Eisenstaedt

Can you make me up to look like someone else, perhaps a movie actor?" Here is the result.

onica Eisenstaedt

Alfred Lorre

son Eisenstaedt

Alfred Bonaparte

Mr. Alfred Hyde

Special Effects

The prop makers were masters of deceit, and so were the optical wizards who used double exposures to create such fancy fakes as a miniature man or a Flying Flivver.

Special-effects men were tricksters. Using clever props, miniature-scale models and doctored film, they could make the most far-fetched fantasies believable. Sometimes they gave substance to the purely imaginary —mermaids, genies, flying cars. At other times they performed prodigies to mimic reality: they dumped tons of water on the actors in *Lifeboat (page 163)* and built a Welsh mining village for *How Green Was My Valley (page 185)* so substantial that it was reused two years later as a Norwegian scene in John Steinbeck's *The Moon Is Down* (1943).

In Mr. Peabody and the Mermaid (1948), Ann Blyth sports a finny finial of rubber, fitted by matching it to a mold of her nether extremities.

Behind the scenes in 1963, John Dominis photographed a stagehand, Atlas-like, carrying a pair of massive boulders. They were made of foam rubber.

The fiberglass horse-halves that sandwich this Civil-War-garbed stunt man floated down a river as two casualties of a battle in Major Dundee (1965).

Gigantic props like these 400-pound scissors and 21-foot pencil created the illusion of a dwindling hero in The Incredible Shrinking Man (1957).

Enraptured by love, Fred Astaire dances up the walls and across the ceiling in Royal Wedding (1951). LIFE, the spoilsport, revealed that his levitation was accomplished by anchoring camera, cameraman and furniture to the floor and rotating the set through 360 degrees while only the dancer remained upright.

A meticulous scale model of Golden Gate Bridge and San Francisco Bay was built by the Japanese makers of the holocaust thriller, 41 Hours of Terror (1960). After the model-builders applied the finishing touches, explosives crumpled their handiwork (below) with satisfactorily apocalyptic effect.

In 1956 LIFE's Allan Grant created his own special effect: a tight-rope walker balancing high above a valley. Actually Grant, from on high, had photographed a technician walking across a painted backdrop set on the ground for measuring and retouching.

By first photographing Sabu, then reducing the picture and finally superimposing the close-up of a genie's foot, special-effects men created this near-crushing scene in The Thief of Bagdad (1940).

A monster's frustrated desire is evoked by superimposing Ingrid Bergman over Spencer Tracy's giant eye in Dr. Jekyll and Mr. Hyde (1941).

Images from two cameras, processed in the laboratory into a single film, reduced Russ Tamblyn to the tiny hero of Tom Thumb (1958), dancing on a drum before a normal-sized princess, June Thorburn.

In The Absent-Minded Professor (1961), Fred MacMurray invented a goo called flubber that made his flivver fly —another tricky superimposition shot.

Seeing Double

*Unsung stand-ins replaced their star-studded lookalikes in
practically every tough studio chore except acting—
and its more rewarding consequences: fame and fortune.*

◀ *Spencer Tracy's double, Roy Thomas, was the object
of an M-G-M manhunt to promote* The Seventh Cross
*(1944). Whoever spotted Thomas in his wanderings
from city to city received a $500 war bond.*

*Mary Lou Isleib (left) was no dead ringer for Shirley
Temple, but she had the same coloring—important for
light measurement. The two, both 16 years old here,
began working together as 7-year-olds.*

*Hazel-eyed Carol Ann Saunders (right), who doubled
for Margaret O'Brien in all her movies, whiles away the
between-takes hours reading and playing games with
the then 6-year-old star.*

Paulette Goddard (left) and stand-in June Kilgour doubled a familiar pin-up pose for this publicity shot. Unlike most stand-ins, June occasionally earned her own billing in minor speaking parts.

The unmistakable ski-slide nose and roving eyes made Jack Robbins (left) a natural double for Bob Hope. Robbins was also noted for his near-perfect mimicry of Hope's stand-up comedy style.

When this photograph appeared, in 1944, Dorothy Panter (left) had been Ginger Rogers' stand-in for seven years. That meant a lot of dyeing because she changed the color of her hair every time Ginger did.

Sylvia Lamarr (left) did her first doubling for Joan Crawford, then was switched to Hedy Lamarr. The fact that she had the same last name may have had something to do with the studio's move.

THE RISE AND FALL OF THE STARS

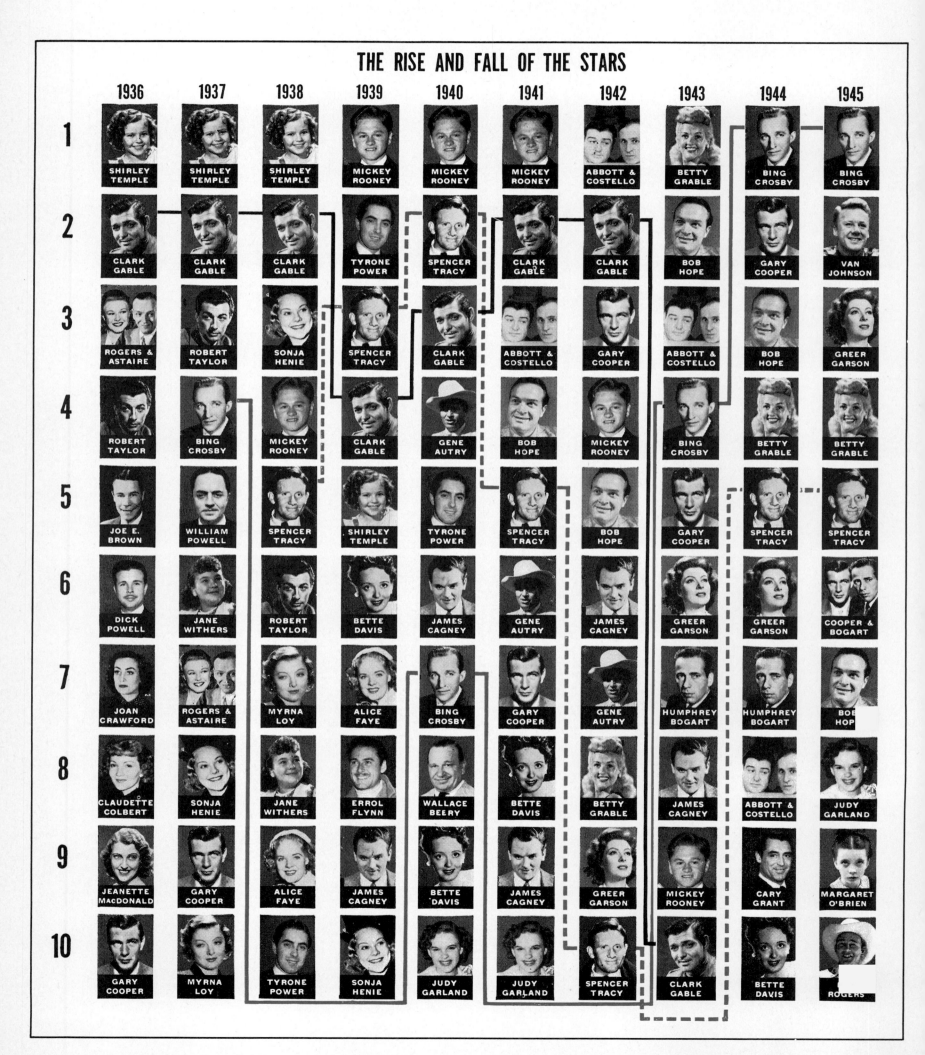

234

The Front Office

*The system worked like a charm until political and labor
troubles erupted, coast-to-coast television arrived,
and a rebellious public refused to eat any more pabulum.*

In 1946 the Hollywood establishment peaked. Box-office grosses reached $1.69 billion— a record. A half-dozen legendary bosses reigned, almost as if by divine right, over the major studios where the production lines were churning out 600 feature films a year. The Star System was humming: scores of indentured players became household gods, and the postwar public was willing to pay to see any movie, no matter how dull or dreary, so long as the name over the title was Clark Gable or Betty Grable or Bing Crosby.

The complacent feeling around the studios was that the prosperity and the system would continue forever. But a palace revolution was already in the making that would alter the industry forever. The portents of change were many: the advent of television, rising costs, a suddenly fickle public, a throttling censorship code; their cumulative effect on the studios was devastating. One major cause was the wave of strikes that periodically held up production, pushed costs even higher and eroded the power of the front-office monarchs. A classic example of the petty jurisdictional squabbles of the time was the burning question of which labor force would make falsies for women's costumes. The prop makers resolved that confrontation with a Solomon-like decree: the costumers would make cloth falsies, while the foam-rubber variety would be the exclusive purview of the make-up artists.

The Motion Picture Production Code, a rigid, often ridiculous system of self-censorship, was another factor in the ultimate downfall of the existing order. The moguls voluntarily girdled the industry with this chastity belt in 1934, and the result was a parade of bland and sterilized movies with the plots prettied up and passions drained out. Outright defiance meant not getting the MPPC's Seal of Approval, and that meant oblivion for a film, because most of the country's exhibitors had sworn allegiance to the code. A historic controversy raged when the censor demanded the alteration of Rhett Butler's famous exit line to Scarlett O'Hara, in *Gone With the Wind:* "Frankly, my dear, I don't give a damn." The last word was to become "darn." The censors lost, Clark Gable uttered the naughty word with relish, and the world survived.

Politics produced a reign of terror in filmdom in 1947 when Congressman J. Parnell Thomas and his House Un-American Activities Committee decided to look for communists in Hollywood and subversive material in films. The hearings made headlines, but the findings were inconclusive. Writers and directors went to jail for refusing to testify, and many careers were ruined or blighted by the ensuing blacklist drawn up by the frightened studio heads. As an ironic postscript to the HUAC inquisition, Chairman Thomas himself went to prison for padding his Congressional payrolls in 1949.

In 1951 the first coast-to-coast television broadcast occurred and nationwide TV became an everyday reality. By 1952 the major studios had bowed to the Department of Justice and agreed to sell their theater chains—a mortal blow to mediocrity, since the moviemakers no longer controlled their own showcases in which to display their wares regardless of quality. By the early '60s most of the old studio despots had ridden into the sunset, and the services of independent producers, directors and stars who could turn out quality films were being sought madly, for enormous fees. The pabulum party was over, the establishment was in shambles and, as LIFE noted, an incredible phenomenon was taking place in Hollywood: "The movies are growing up."

The durability of certain box-office champions is demonstrated by the fact that only 36 faces appeared in the 100 popularity rankings covering the golden decade before the decline and fall of the studio system. The ups and downs and ups of three famous careers were tracked on this 1948 LIFE chart.

235

Trouble in Dreamland

*Immediately after World War II, strikes and a blundering
Congressional hunt for communists, both harbingers
of the end of big-studio prestige, shook Hollywood badly.*

A deputy sheriff swings his night stick at a striking trade-unionist in a 1946 jurisdictional dispute. A wave of confrontations began the year before.

Fred Astaire talks to an idle actress in a 1960 shutdown he called "violently wrong."

In the same walkout, a picket pummels a nonstriker who wanted to cross the line.

Behind a cloud of smoke, Adolphe Menjou testifies before the House Un-American Activities Committee that director John Cromwell had told him "Capitalism is through."

Craning for a better view at a Washington hearing, Danny Kaye, June Havoc, Humphrey Bogart and Lauren Bacall represent a group that charged HUAC with violating civil rights.

An uneasy HUAC witness, Robert Taylor responds to questioning by naming three writers as communists. He immediately added, "Of course I wouldn't know, personally."

237

The Winds of Change

Television mania (and bad movies) turned theaters into supermarkets, and studio heads who were once monarchs yielded their thrones to their former subjects, the stars.

In August 1951, noting that 3,000 movie houses had shut down within a year and that receipts were at their lowest level in two decades, the editors ran pictures of a Detroit theater for rent and a New York house already converted to business use.

To illustrate a 1957 article by Eric Hodgins on the new Hollywood, the famed caricaturist of entertainers, Al Hirschfeld, concocted a representative scene in which an old-style studio boss, while mindlessly snipping away at the product, accepted the obscene fawning of satraps, hangers-on and compliant starlets.

L. B. Mayer (foreground), autocratic boss of M-G-M, meets with studio executives in 1948 to stem the drain of profits prestige and power with which the industry was being confronted. Three years later he resigned; mighty Metro was never the same again.

In contrast with the old look (opposite page), Hirschfeld's interpretation of the talent take-over featured five stars, surrounded by flunkies, while the same studio boss curried favor: (from left, clockwise) Frank Sinatra, Marlon Brando, Gary Cooper, Marilyn Monroe, Kirk Douglas and Burt Lancaster.

Motorcades of movie-goers filled a San Francisco drive-in to see *Beyond the Valley of the Dolls* (1970), the first high-budget—$2 million—sex film, directed by Russ Meyer, "King of the Nudies." But Meyer's "skin flicks" were demure in comparison to the explicit pornography that hit the fans the same year.

As *Baby Doll* (1956), Carroll Baker played the child-woman bride of a man who had agreed not to touch her until her 20th birthday. The first shocking view of *Baby Doll*—in an oversized crib, sucking her thumb—helped bring about the alphabetical system of rating films for family acceptability.

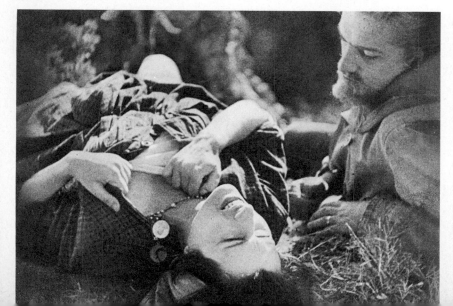

Clearly labeled under the newly revised Code of Self-Regulation a pornucopia of stag films was now free to burst forth, flaunting their X ratings as attractive come-ons. California pornographer Matt Cimber (right) ground out The Sensuous Female (1970) in two weeks for $85,000, and cleaned up at the box office.

In The Miracle (1951), from Italy, Anna Magnani played a goat girl who gave herself to a vagrant she believed to be St. Joseph. Efforts to ban the movie in the U.S. failed when the Supreme Court, holding that "sacrilegious" was a term too ambiguous to be enforced, extended freedom of press and speech to films.

Mingling with cast and crew on the sound stages, LIFE suggested new ideas, invented new approaches and borrowed the actors for its own stories. The magazine also followed the stars to their parties, went home with them, and watched them raise their children and grow old. (A few were even followed all the way to jail.)

Behind the Scenes

So much did LIFE inject itself into the many aspects of the Hollywood scene that it was sometimes difficult to tell the staffers from the supporting players on the set or the revelers at Chasen's. From the first, the magazine's reporter-photographer teams covered movies and moviemakers with a devotion and an intensity that came as a surprise to film folk accustomed to flights of fan-magazine fancy and the peephole journalism of the scandal sheets and gossip columns.

Though as a rule they were self-effacing, accepting the time-honored role of invisibility, the journalists sometimes not only made the scene but also set it. Shooting his still pictures for *Yellow Sky (page 251),* John Florea wangled from the movie's crew huge amounts of space, time and cooperation—plus two mammoth seamless paper backdrops (a blue one for night and a yellow one for day) against which he had decided to photograph a stylized version of the script. To do so, he borrowed the very actors director William Wellman had cast. Scene by scene, as the movie was shot, first the cameras rolled on the set and the actors played their parts—and then everything came to a halt while the performers rushed over to Florea's neighboring set to re-do the same scene for LIFE. It didn't take long for this arrangement to irk Wellman. Recalled Florea: "He kept protesting, 'Who the hell is directing this show, me or Florea?' "

It became a typical complaint. Yet many of LIFE's ingenious ideas proved serendipitous, with the movies adapting a still-picture composition or concept that originated in the magazine—as Florea's stylized sets inspired a later Western musical, *Red Garters (page 251).* The directors, therefore, did not complain too bitterly; the smarter ones watched the journalists at work, on the odds-on chance that there might be some mutually rewarding cross-fertilization.

Some staffers became so good at producing movie ideas that they turned to producing movies—period. The most famous such LIFE graduate was Gordon Parks. For a 1963 LIFE assignment, the multi-talented Parks wrote and photographed the poignant and adventurous segment of his autobiography that dealt with growing up black in the Middle West of the 1920s. After the essay appeared in the magazine, Parks wrote, directed and created the musical score for a film version of his book *The Learning Tree* (1969), which made his reputation—and his fortune—as a Renaissance man of moviedom. Other LIFE photographers who turned producer were Florea, and Allan Grant, who took the picture of Russ Tamblyn flipping over his girl friend on page 282. Grant made a series of satirical comedy shorts in the late 1940s and early '50s, culminating in *Six O'Clock Low,* a devastating put-on of 1950's

tough look at Air Force brass in World War II, *Twelve O'Clock High.* Not content with penetrating the movie sets, LIFE's photographers followed the stars right into their private lives. Many of the magazine's Hollywood crew could count a star or two among their close friends. Reporter Stanley Flink, who had learned in confidence the many reasons for Marilyn Monroe's towering insecurity long before the story of her earliest years became common knowledge, found himself serving protectively for a time as a combination chauffeur-confidant, squiring her to parties and seeing that she was on time for photography sessions and interviews (particularly LIFE photography sessions and interviews). At one party he caught her so often when she tripped over her more than usually ankle-tight skirt that she called him "my catcher."

On occasion a staffer also contributed to the complications attending the industry's social life. Reporter David Zeitlin recalls that he introduced a relatively unknown starlet named Mia Farrow to not-so-unknown Frank Sinatra. It was 1966, on the set of *Von Ryan's Express,* and Mia was visiting a former boy friend. Zeitlin asked her if she had met Mr. Sinatra; the future Mrs. Sinatra said she hadn't. Zeitlin rectified that—unaware that he was contributing to pop history.

Most of the magazine's involvement with the stars in their off-screen firmament was less personal. At the big Hollywood parties, of which there were plenty, the editors could cover hundreds of the great and near-great in the course of a single evening—and regularly did, under the heading "LIFE Goes to a Party" *(pages 278-279).* At these big bashes Hollywood was its most Hollywoodish, and the stars seemed to be putting in overtime to preserve the illusions of their fans. On such occasions the editors liked to report such oddments as the fact that Gene Tierney wore a $14 dress to a $50,000 costume ball *(opposite),* lending savor to the display of the rest of the party-goers, who appeared to be trying their best to behave like the very famous people they were.

But through it all, and despite its iconoclastic approach to the actual movies, LIFE managed to maintain an affectionate and faintly awestruck attitude toward the famous toilers of the dream factories. Even when Hollywood came upon difficult times and much of the glamor began to go, LIFE helped to keep alive the legend of a select group of very beautiful people who had entertained, inspired and delighted us poor mortals, both on the big screen and in the pages of the big magazine.

Four covers catch the variety of LIFE in Hollywood: Paulette Goddard at private ease, Gene Tierney at play, Rex Harrison and his talented wife on vacation, and Shirley MacLaine clowning with her daughter.

LIFE

PAULETTE GODDARD

APRIL 18, 1938 **10** CENTS

REG. U. S. PAT. OFF.

LIFE

IN THIS ISSUE
POPE PIUS—BY GRAHAM GREENE

GENE TIERNEY WEARS $14 DRESS
TO A $50,000 PARTY IN VENICE

20 CENTS
SEPTEMBER 24, 1951
CIRCULATION OVER
5,200,000

REG. U. S. PAT. OFF.

LIFE

CRIME IV: EXCLUSIVE PHOTOGRAPHS
INSIDE PRISON, TAKEN BY A CONVICT

KAY KENDALL
AND HUSBAND
REX HARRISON

20 CENTS
SEPTEMBER 30, 1957

LIFE

FLORIDA'S MAIL ORDER LAND RUSH

NEW LINCOLN FIND RECALLS DAYS
IN SPRINGFIELD WITH HIS NEIGHBORS

THE SAUCY MacLAINES:
SHIRLEY AND DAUGHTER

FEBRUARY 9, 1959 **25** CENTS

The Editorial Influence

Taking full advantage of its symbiotic relationship with filmdom, the magazine frequently swapped talents with the moviemakers. Everyone came out ahead of the game.

When the magazine proposed to do a special issue on the movies in 1963, Associate Editor Mary Leatherbee, the talented younger sister of producer Joshua Logan, came up with the idea of having the stars re-create movie highlights of the past. The big question, of course, was: How do you get the highest-paid people in Hollywood to put on such demanding free performances? Mary decided that if she could get one of the biggest and best established stars to cooperate, the others would in all probability follow his lead. So she telephoned Cary Grant and put it to him directly: Would he play Charlie Chaplin for a LIFE photographer? Grant's immediate response was no.

But he figured without Mary's legendary wheedling ability. She subjected him to a full hour of sweet persistence and enthusiasm. Grant capitulated. And in his wake, as Mary had reasoned, so did all the other luminaries she approached with the word that Grant had already agreed to cooperate. When he appeared for his own photographing session —outfitted with baggy pants, moustache and cane—Grant reminded Mary of her emotion-filled phone call and handed her a package wrapped with a velvet ribbon. "For the most memorable performance of the year," he said. Mary opened it and found an Oscar.

It was a mark of the persuasiveness of LIFE's editors and photographers—and of the magazine's influence with movie fans—that Hollywood almost always went along with their wildest story ideas. No one batted an eye when the staff decided to round up an all-star Keystone Cop police force and restage an old-fashioned Mack Sennett comedy for a 1958 special issue on entertainment, or when photographer Richard Avedon coaxed Marilyn Monroe into re-creating the silent sirens and voluptuous vamps of earlier times as an exercise in nostalgia for the same issue.

In fact, so many actresses and would-be actresses posed for photographer Eliot Elisofon that, as early as 1942, he collected them for a one-man show. In the process he noted a bit of previously neglected Hollywood sociology: the warning around the film capital was "Don't get yourself an actress for a girl friend"—because she'll always scoot home no later than 9 o'clock in order to look well for the camera the next morning.

In 1949, Alfred Eisenstaedt, not content with photographing the movie greats, conceived the idea of imitating them himself. He thereupon coaxed movie make-up magician Wally Westmore to change him from a photographer into a good imitation of everyone from Groucho Marx to Veronica Lake. The results can be seen on pages 222-223.

If LIFE tended to use Hollywood's stars and its facilities as if they were the magazine's own, there was more than a little repayment: the industry frequently got more than publicity in exchange. Photographs from LIFE often reappeared in nearly exact duplicate in movies, and articles in the magazine occasionally provided the basis for entire films. Sometimes, as in *The Grapes of Wrath* in 1939 and *This Above All* in 1942, the retelling in stills of a current book inspired Hollywood's treatment, right down to ideas for characterizations and scenery.

The studios were also known to attempt reversing the talent-borrowing process. In 1943 photographer Marie Hansen was offered a screen test. Carefully coiffed and heavily made up, she went through an emotional test scene with Walter Pidgeon, and producer Joseph Pasternak was sufficiently impressed to offer her a contract. Marie's report of her decision was brief: "I wasn't too tempted by it."

A hot-blooded sheik (is it Rudolph Valentino?) admires his catch (Vilma Banky?) before whisking her off to his desert hideaway. Tony Curtis and Natalie Wood were among the stars the magazine corralled to re-create in fun the romance of a long-gone era.

Filmed from LIFE

With almost uncanny verisimilitude, the movies copied news events, situations and even props from the picture magazine, right down to the pictures themselves.

In 1947 LIFE ran the picture above of a beer-drinking motorcyclist who with his friends invaded Hollister, California. The story prompted Stanley Kramer to re-create the incident in The Wild One (1953); at right, Lee Marvin, a rival of Marlon Brando's Black Rebels, strikes a brazen pose echoing the real thing.

When Marine Al Schmid came home from Guadalcanal in 1943, blinded by a grenade, his faithful girl friend was waiting to marry him, and LIFE photographed them on their front porch (left). Above, John Garfield recreates Schmid—and Eleanor Parker, his wife—on a duplicate set, in Pride of the Marines (1945).

The heroism of Army nurses in the Philippines was documented in a 1942 story that included a photograph (below, left) by LIFE correspondent Melville Jacoby, who was later killed in action. Paramount put their experiences on film in So Proudly We Hail (1943), carefully copying Jacoby's camera record.

Pier Angeli (below) was lured off the studio lot by Allan Grant in 1954 and provided with a rented deer for his magazine interpretation of Rima, the bird-girl of the jungle in W. H. Hudson's novel, Green Mansions. Hollywood got around to filming the book in 1959—but with Audrey Hepburn (right).

RAMEYVILLE
BANK

HOU
10:00 A
4:00

While Gregory Peck and Richard Widmark were making *Yellow Sky* (1948), a standard Western, John Florea photographed a spoof of it with minimal props (above). The musical *Red Garters* (1954) included a Western parody, with scenes like this gunfight (left) shot on similarly designed sets.

Old Pros in New Roles

The stars were reluctant when LIFE asked them to re-create oldtime movies and the roles of earlier stars. But once they got started, they gave it their hilarious best.

Fresh off the Charade set, the usually dapper Cary Grant tramped in as Chaplin to help bring back an earlier era for the 1963 LIFE movie issue.

Jack Lemmon revived the World War I dogfight movie by playing an American ace meeting his match somewhere in the skies over France.

Paul Newman helped bring back the good old days of derring-do by mimicking Douglas Fairbanks as a great swashbuckler: Don Juan, Zorro, D'Artagnan and the Thief of Bagdad rolled into one.

In a scene not quite straight out of Ben-Hur, two of the grinningest charioteers in history, Frank Sinatra and Dean Martin, switched to grimaces while racing hell for leather in muddied chariots.

253

Bob Hope and Bing Crosby, off this time on the road to Chicago, do their deadpan impression of a 1930s-style gangster-movie massacre, with guns blazing and an unprecedented lack of harmony.

A star cast acts out LIFE's script of a Mack Sennett-style comedy. Preceding photographs had shown Rock Hudson kidnaping his sweetheart, Kim Novak, as she was about to become Paul Newman's unwilling bride. Here the villain and frenetic Keystone Cops seek the fugitives, hiding among beach beauties.

Don Murray

Nick Adams   **Tommy Sands**

Debbie Reynolds   **Shirley MacLaine**   **Marge Champion**   **Sheree North**   **Rock Huds**

Fess Parker   Gower Champion   Paul Newman

                  Buddy Ebsen   James Garner

Kim Novak   Lee Remick   Dana Wynter   Joan Collins

Private Lives

Their romances were colorful, their divorces Byzantine in complexity. Underneath it all, the stars had the same hopes, fears and problems as other people—only more so.

Hollywood's famous—even the very, very famous—worked, played, married, had children and grew old like their fans. But there was a difference: the stars in their courses were bathed in the steady, hot light of publicity. To pursue any private existence at all required titanic, Garboesque determination.

Many big names went happily along with the interest of fans and press—which of course coincided with the interest of studio press relations. They gave interviews gracefully about their hobbies, their hubbies and their babies. LIFE's Ed Clark was welcomed at author Louis Bromfield's rambling Ohio farmhouse to record the marriage there of Bogey and his Baby in 1945 *(page 263).* Alfred Eisenstaedt followed Shirley Temple almost from cradle to Congressional campaign, starting with a photograph of the dimpled tot that he took in early 1936, just before LIFE was born, and progressing to a dignified 1965 portrait of Mrs. Black with her debutante daughter *(page 269).*

Peter Stackpole spent days with Joan Bennett and her family in 1940, even catching mother and child at naptime *(page 266).* Though they didn't quite come across as your typical down-to-earth folks next door, they were clearly an affectionate menage.

Some stars resisted publicity simply because of their personalities. Reporter Jim Lebenthal described Fred Astaire as one of the most reserved, shy people he had ever met. "He's almost unbelievably modest," said Lebenthal in some surprise. Fred's private life was indeed his own, and he tried to keep it that way; rarely did a writer create a portrait of him in depth, as Lincoln Barnett did in 1941. In it, Barnett also took an intimate look at Adele, Lady Cavendish, who was Fred's sister and his original dancing partner; and

Astaire's wife and children got fuller coverage than they had had nearly anywhere else. Bob Landry's cover picture, showing Fred and his son dancing *(page 266),* was one of the few photographs of his family that Astaire ever permitted. It may have had something to do with the fact that Barnett himself was an amateur tap dancer.

But reserve was not the only reason for the stars' reticence. Some were downright hostile to the press. The picture on the facing page notwithstanding, Steve McQueen so little liked intrusions on his privacy that he once reacted to the penetrating questions of LIFE's Tommy Thompson by demanding that the editors send another reporter in Thompson's place. They did. But a later McQueen-LIFE confrontation came out differently. McQueen kept bureau chief Jon Frook cooling his heels for about 10 days, first during a visit to Cape Cod and then back in Los Angeles, waiting for a promised interview. Frook finally walked off and went back to his other work.

It sometimes appeared that the subjects who were the least publicity-shy had the most tangled lives. The Eddie-Debbie-Liz-Richard romantic marathon, for example, was documented in minute detail by the world's press —with the magazine in the vanguard—from the time "The Widow Todd," as LIFE called Elizabeth Taylor in 1958, began dating Eddie Fisher *(pages 270-271)* until Burton and Taylor were at last wed. LIFE, in fact, was one of only two publications that were permitted to cover the 1964 marriage ceremony of Cleopatra and her Antony, in Montreal. Still, conversing candidly with associate editor Dick Meryman later in the same year, Liz protested: "Believe it or not, to my kids, I'm not Elizabeth Taylor at all; I'm not anybody other than 'Mommy.' " It was not so hard to believe.

In Palm Springs, Steve McQueen and his wife, Neile, assume a conjugal attitude. The 1963 article that accompanied this John Dominis photograph was one of McQueen's infrequent interviews.

259

To Each His Own Bliss

Pastimes ranged from acquiring art to pool tables—or swimming pools—but the favorite, and often enough the most lasting, hobbies seemed to be love and marriage.

Victor Moore and feathered friend cavort in 1947 in his ▶ Beverly Hills backyard pool. The diving duck, complete with bathing suit, was a gift from Mrs. Moore.

Edward G. Robinson exhibits (from top) a Rouault, a Bonnard and a Vuillard, three of 14 paintings left after he sold most of his huge art collection in 1957. Ship-owner Stavros Niarchos was the top bidder.

After a hard day on his toes in 1941, Fred Astaire faces a mammoth filing job as he smoothes the taps on some of his 84 pairs of dancing shoes. Each pair lasted for perhaps half a dozen filming sessions.

Tony Curtis was photographed by Ralph Crane looming symbolically above his new 1961 Rolls-Royce to emphasize that after 39 movies the erstwhile kid from the Bronx had really made good in Hollywood.

Ingrid Bergman and director Roberto Rossellini stroll hand in hand on the volcanic island of Stromboli in 1949, far from the world press rumblings in reaction to their not-yet-legalized liaison.

Joanne Woodward (Mrs. Paul Newman) rests on her hubby, as well as her laurels, after filming Rachel, Rachel (1968), which he directed. Their marriage proved as enduring as it was endearing to fans.

Lauren Bacall, 20, feeds wedding cake to her new husband, Humphrey Bogart. It was the "Picture of the Week" in LIFE's issue dated June 4, 1945.

Author Roald Dahl gives roses to his wife, Patricia Neal, in 1965. She had suffered a stroke five months earlier and was carrying their fifth child.

Jimmy Stewart's grin is appropriate at his marriage in 1949 to Gloria Hatrick MacLean. She had recently divorced the son of the Hope Diamond's owner.

In 1964 Sophia Loren hugs husband Carlo Ponti in gratitude. He had just presented her with a magnificent 16th Century villa nestled in the hills near Rome.

The Children's Hour

The publicity prattle that came with their rattle was noisier for star-babies than others, and as the kids grew up some inevitably reached for their own identity.

Lana Turner holds her daughter, Cheryl Crane, in 1944. *"Defending her mother"* 14 years later, Cheryl killed Lana's mobster-lover (page 297).

One-year-old Vicky is not much taller than her cake as she blows out the sole candle in 1944, watched by proud parents Betty Grable and Harry James.

Pier Angeli laughs at her son Perry during a happy moment in 1956. Two years later she was fighting with husband Vic Damone for Perry's custody. ▶

BB's bébé flashes a smile as big as his mother's. Young Nicholas Charrier, born in 1960, was Brigitte Bardot's child by actor Jacques Charrier.

Born in January 1950, four-day-old Yasmin sleeps soundly between her happy mother, Rita Hayworth, and her father, Prince Aly Khan.

A month old in April 1961, John Clark Gable waves from mother's arms with the savoir-faire of his dad, who had died of a coronary five months earlier.

A squirming Robertino Rossellini upstages mother Ingrid Bergman. His parents were married by proxy in Mexico shortly after his birth in 1950.

265

Reading to her daughter Melinda after finishing work on *The Man I Married* (1940), Joan Bennett curls up on her little girl's Hollywood bed.

In 1953 LIFE reached back 22 years into Marlene Dietrich's family album to show her with her 5-year-old daughter Maria Riva. By 1953 Maria was 26, an actress in her own right and a mother.

Learning a bit of the old soft shoe from his father in 1941, 5-year-old Fred Astaire Jr. preferred his own side-saddle technique to that of his dad. His mother was Boston socialite Phyllis Potter.

Henry Fonda shows off daughter Jane and son Peter in 1941. Jane was 3 and relatively docile then, and Peter was an easy rider only in papa's lap.

Shirley MacLaine and daughter Stephanie, 6, share a wide-mouthed appreciation of the delights of Paris during the filming of Irma La Douce (1963).

Nita Bieber (below), who was a graceful hopeful at M-G-M, coaches her young nephew Christopher in a barely adequate arabesque for LIFE in 1949.

Absorbed in her own whirl, Lorna Luft swings into an impromptu routine while her mother, Judy Garland, is rehearsing for a TV special in 1955.

The most tangled family tree in Hollywood was the shifting ménage of Fisher, Reynolds,

Singer Eddie Fisher, 26, began dating actress Debbie Reynolds, 22, in 1954, while a chorus of U.S. bobby-soxers shrilled, "Say it isn't so, Eddie."

One day in September 1955, the Debbie-Eddie romance ended in a swap of "I do"s at Grossingers. Next day, back on tour, they admired her new ring.

By 1958 the family was a foursome, now including Carrie, 1½, and Todd, two months. Todd was named for good friend Mike Todd, Liz Taylor's husband.

The Todds and the Fishers, a companionable foursome, made joint appearances at such public places as England's Epsom Downs in 1957.

270

Todd, Taylor, and Burton, to say nothing of their understandably bewildered children.

Then, in 1958, Todd was killed. Consoling Liz in New York six months later, Eddie missed his plane home —by a week. A year after, they were a pair.

A month later, flying home from Europe, Debbie was greeted by daughter Carrie and by newsmen full of questions about Eddie and Liz and divorce.

After Debbie announced that she would okay a Nevada divorce, Eddie and Liz embraced. "I knew she would. Chalk it up to intuition," said Mrs. Todd.

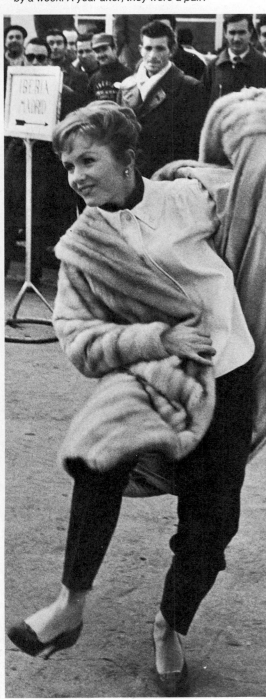

On a 1962 visit to the Cleopatra set in Rome, Eddie played king to queenly Liz, now his wife. She was also a good friend of Richard Burton (Antony).

Of her friendship with Burton (left), Liz told LIFE: "The way I began falling in love with Richard was funny." Eddie did not seem to agree.

Acting not at all like a woman scorned, Debbie, on location in Madrid, flicked her mink in a bullfighter's pass, threw kisses and caused traffic jams.

With divorce from Eddie, the romance between Antony and Cleopatra ripened into marriage between Richard and Liz—and ultimately into divorce.

The March of Time

Only the celluloid self could be young forever; but the best of the movie people proved that age need not wither nor custom stale the appeal that had made them stars.

At 44 in 1960, Betty Grable takes an old pose in front of one of her wartime pin-up pictures, proving the years had not made her much fuller of figure.

In 1965, Fred Astaire betrays some weariness as he uses a practice bar for support while working out a new dance routine. Still, at 66 he could rehearse longer than most of the younger dancers.

The stone profile of Buster Keaton reveals some granitic lines as he ruminates between takes of a Samuel Beckett movie called Film (1965). He was 69.

Vivien Leigh at 48 shows in The Roman Spring of Mrs. Stone (1961) that she could look as well as play the part of a lady on whom age sits lightly.

◀ The 60-year-old Cary Grant looks every bit his age as a beach bum in his 71st movie, Father Goose (1964). The Grant charm still showed through.

At 55 and 53, Lillian (left) and Dorothy Gish sit for a 1951 portrait to match one made in 1914 when they were working for D. W. Griffith. The comparison showed that age had but mellowed their beauty.

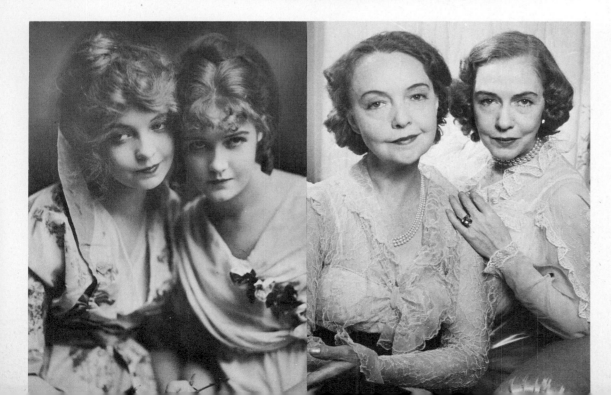

The Showcase

A Hollywood personality was a public personality, and worked hard at it even in play. There were many reasons, not the least being a star's natural reaction to a camera.

Every Hollywood star worth the sparkle knew that whether or not he was on the set, he was almost always on camera. And in many cases an actor or actress reacted to the sight of a camera the way a trout does to a fly; it was an automatic response.

This simple rule of Hollywood behavior was proved, in a reverse way, by one Texas millionaire who decided to give a party in the movie capital. When the host refused to admit photographers, a friend hinted that movie people did not like to get all dressed up and *not* be photographed. So the Texan agreed to let the photographers in for an hour and a half. The party was a dull affair—until the cameramen arrived *(pages 278-279).*

Most movie stars—and all movie starlets —would usually drop whatever they were doing to go along with an intriguing publicity stunt. Maria Montez happily helped LIFE spoof Hollywood's craze for physical fitness by jogging with W. C. Fields *(page 283).* The exercise session quickly recessed for drinks, with Fields imbibing rum from a glass with a wooden lid, designed, as Fields explained, to "keep out the flies." Maria mentioned that her recent sweater picture in LIFE had drawn 300 letters. Fields pondered that, then suggested: "I s'pose a lotta people have never been weaned."

For a Halloween party in 1947, Ingrid Bergman decided to masquerade as a witch. She made herself up until she was satisfied she was absolutely unrecognizable, and allowed a photographer to record the transformation *(page 282).* In her disguise she could not resist the temptation to pay a call on Alfred Hitchcock, who was ailing and confined to bed. "When Mrs. Hitchcock answered the door," recalls Joe Steele, Ingrid's agent at the time, "we signaled her not to say anything, and she took us up to the master's bedroom. Hitchcock was lying there with his eyes closed. He opened them, took one glance at the witch hovering over him, and said, calmly, 'What are you doing here, Ingrid?' "

World War II provided an excellent opportunity for the stars to perform a double service: cheer up the men in uniform and attract publicity while doing so, thereby entertaining the millions of additional servicemen who read about their activities. One indefatigable trouper to the troops was Bob Hope, who in a single tour with Frances Langford covered 80,000 miles visiting GIs at their bases away from home. Reminiscing about the trip later, Hope reported: "It got so hot in Sicily that we thought we'd be more comfortable if we did our shows in shorts. Frances was the first to try it. What an inspiration a pair of Hollywood legs were to those men! A few days later Italy surrendered." When he was about to leave on a bomber flight, Hope was asked whom he wished to be notified in case of accident. He named Louella Parsons as his next of kin. "She'd be mad," he explained, "if she wasn't the first to know."

Louella and the other all-powerful gossip columnists were, of course, as finely attuned to publicity as the stars themselves. And for reasons not difficult to divine, the stars often helped the columnists with their own publicity. In 1941 Hedda Hooper packed up her dozens of screwball hats and moved from the eight-room bungalow she had lived in for 17 years to a Beverly Hills home that better reflected her national eminence. When she threw a house-moving party, Cary Grant was among those who came along to help with the lugging *(page 289).* In later years "The Hat" was not above pointing to her mansion and chortling, "That's the house that fear built."

Marlene Dietrich manages a lovely laugh in response to a Noel Coward bon mot at the Metropolitan Opera House's Louis Sherry bar during the intermission of the Bolshoi Ballet's U.S. premiere in 1959.

275

"Among Those Present . . ."

Aware that dullness is the unforgivable show-business sin, Hollywood luminaries brought their special, if professional, exuberance to any gala they graced.

Ginger Rogers and Ann Miller enhance their status as hoofers at a party during the height of Hollywood's 1950 re-infatuation with the Charleston.

From the tips of her toes to the tops of her tonsils, Martha Raye gives her all in an exhibition of the cancan during a 1939 Edgar Bergen party celebrating his famous wooden side-kick, Charlie McCarthy.

At Darryl Zanuck's party for his daughter in 1954, the host steals the show by chinning himself with one hand as he swings on a trapeze.

Clowning behind a strawberry nose, Bing Crosby treats the audience to a view of his famous tongue during a 1948 charity show in which top stars became big-top stars to raise money for a hospital.

277

Hollywood's parties seemed made to order for LIFE. This one in 1941 was typical—star

Virginia Field & Eddie Bergen contemplate an adagio maneuver. Miss Field, who has worn skirts in all her pictures, enchanted everybody by disclosure of her exceptional legs.

Travis Banton & Hedda Hopper achieve the evening's best concealment. Designer Banton himself just plain "Death." Miss Hopper, unable to breathe, soon had to resume her own ide

Life Goes to a Hollywood Party

Cinema elite attend in costume

In Hollywood Jan. 26, more than 200 movie s press agents and publicity buffs disported t selves at a fancy shindig that offered everythin U. S. fan ever envisaged in the way of a Holly party. It took place at Ciro's. Guests came in lent costumes, glamorously obtained by raiding dio wardrobes. Dorothy Lamour's famous con were present. An Earl Carroll girlie named Wallace bounced pinkly about the floor in one o least constricting ensembles ever seen on a Jan evening. Champagne burbled in high tidal a

Rudy Vallée & Beryl Wallace talk shop. Beryl, pretty protégée of Earl Carroll, wore only bridal veil, bra, ruffly white panties.

Cobina Wright Jr., guest of honor, sings to obbligato by Emil Coleman's orchestra. She recently completed her first film.

John Randolph Hearst & Anita Louise sit one out. You ablest son of publisher-father, John is with *American We*

nd Russell's hilarity reveals her rear molars to Freddy Brisson, about whom she is reported-at way" but won't admit it. Rosalind appears as a sublimated Quaker girl, trimmed in pink.

Louella Parsons & Earl Carroll get together for a little rug-cutting. Pundit Parsons is dressed as Lillian Russell, Impresario Carroll as Amphitryon, legendary Greek warrior.

e. And the whole affair was hosted by a gentleman m most of guests knew virtually nothing about. he question "Who is Rex St. Cyr?" kept gossips all evening. It was persistently reported that terious Mr. St. Cyr was once plain Jack Thomp-of Waco, Texas; a onetime newsboy, onetime us boy, who married a wealthy widow and in-ed $20,000,000 when she died in 1915, married h divorcée a few months later and inherited 000,000 when *she* died. No one knew what he doing in Hollywood. No one cared. No one knew

exactly why he gave the party—though it was for-mally dedicated to Cobina Wright Jr. (*see cover*) and appeared to be a sort of unofficial debut for her. But virtually everybody who was anybody was there.

To no one did Mr. St. Cyr's hospitality bring a greater enjoyment than to Juanita Stark, 19-year-old "find," whom a Warner Brothers scout had spot-ted on Monday, Jan. 20, as she drew $10 from a relief office in Los Angeles. Screen tested Tuesday, she received a contract Wednesday. For pictures of rapt Juanita at her first big Hollywood party, turn page.

Morgan Vanderbilt as Marie Antoinette has supper with Gaynor and Janet's husband, M-G-M Designer Adrian.

Ruth Hussey, RKO star, flops around comfortably as rag doll. Her reputed fiance, Producer Raphael Hakim, enacts a sheik.

Dorothy Lamour & Host St. Cyr play Sneezy Sneezy with cham-pagne bubbles. Mr. St. Cyr's ruffles are in good gaucho taste.

CONTINUED ON NEXT PAGE 85

Fun and Games

In the pauses after their screen occupations, the actors succeeded in keeping their star images burnished. But they also found the time to indulge in high jinks and low.

Head over heels in love with his fiancée, Venetia Stevenson, in 1955, dancer Russ Tamblyn casually flips for her while strolling down Rodeo Boulevard.

Equipping herself with a lined face, a somber surplice and a nose wart, this lady attends a Halloween party in 1947 as a hag. Her name: Ingrid Bergman.

Arranged to show off her best assets, Jayne Mansfield makes sure she does not arrive unnoticed at a 1956 party, on the arms of Mickey Hargitay.

As if she needed it, Natalie Wood keeps in shape practicing home gymnastics with the help of Dennis Hopper (left) and Nick Adams, who were supposedly helping her study dramatics. The act was a spoof on the then-current (1956) circus movie Trapeze.

Easily outpaced by starlet Maria Montez, W. C. Fields trots along in fine 1941 form, looking almost as if he would rather be jogging in Philadelphia.

Doing Their Bit

*"Something for the boys" was no gag but a passionate
wartime act of faith for stars who trekked through
much of the world to boost morale and sell war bonds.*

*Carefully held aloft by her famous legs, Marlene Die-
trich gives a welcome-home kiss to a lucky member of
the 2nd Division on the arrival of the troopship Mon-
ticello in New York Harbor in 1945.*

*Movie butler Arthur Treacher, who had offered to play
his screen role in real life for the largest purchaser in a
1944 war-bond drive, is led from the auction block on a
lasso by the man who bought $50,000 worth.*

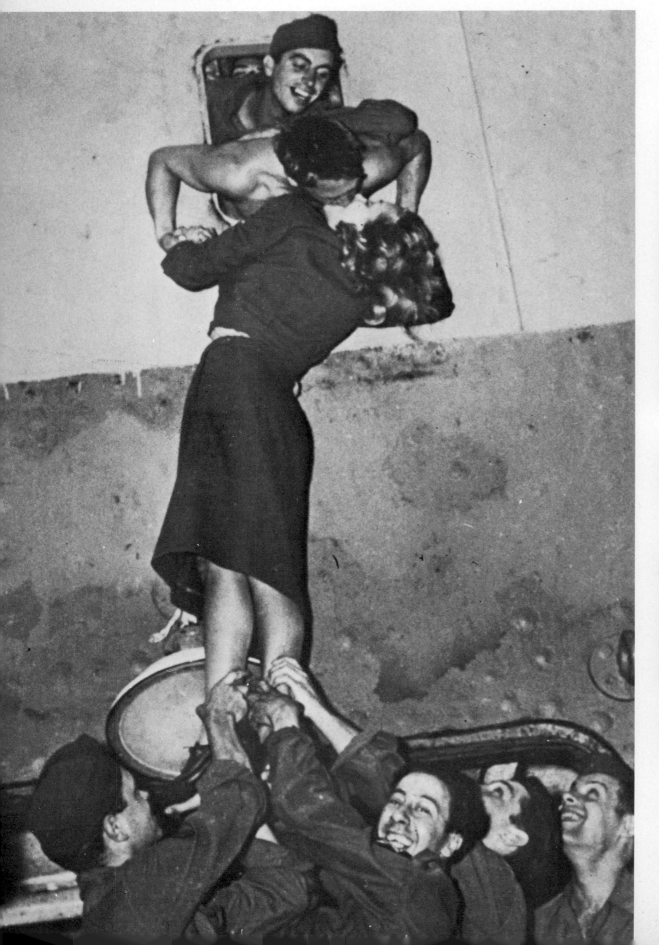

*Hot and sweaty after a vigorous 1943 performance,
rubber-mouthed comedian Joe E. Brown willingly signs
autographs for troops on Guadalcanal.*

*Frances Langford and Bob Hope do an impromptu act ▶
in England in 1944, after finding that their welcoming
committee of one has fallen asleep.*

Rita Hayworth, voted the Away-From-Home Mother of Camp Callan, Calif., in 1942, turns one Private Eklund over her knee to stitch a critical tear.

Wincing while her long blonde trademark becomes entangled in a drill, Veronica Lake does a dramatic demonstration in 1943, at government request, to warn similarly hirsute war-plant workers.

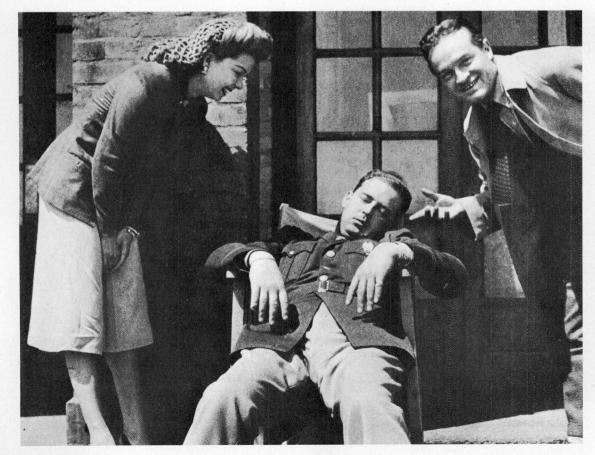

In the uniform of Hollywood's Stage Door Canteen, Claudette Colbert tutors a GI in gin rummy during a 1942 canteen party at Ft. MacArthur, Calif.

285

The Academy Awards

Some of Hollywood's most moving moments were recorded by still photographers covering the emotional scenes at the annual Academy Award presentations.

The blank-faced golden boy of Hollywood, officially called the Academy Award but popularly known as Oscar, has an intrinsic value of about $100. But actors and actresses lust for him: directors, producers and technicians covet him. Winners called to the stage kiss him, wave him at the audience, or become so excited that they drop him. As LIFE's photographers showed in covering the emotional Academy Award ceremonies through the years, Oscar not only rewards Hollywood's best performances; he also elicits a few.

After accepting her award, Joan Fontaine registers the proper decorous awe at the 1941 Oscar she won for Best Performance in her role in Suspicion.

Simone Signoret strains to hear if her part in Room at the Top (1959) has won her the Oscar. Moments later she knew it had, and rushed to the stage.

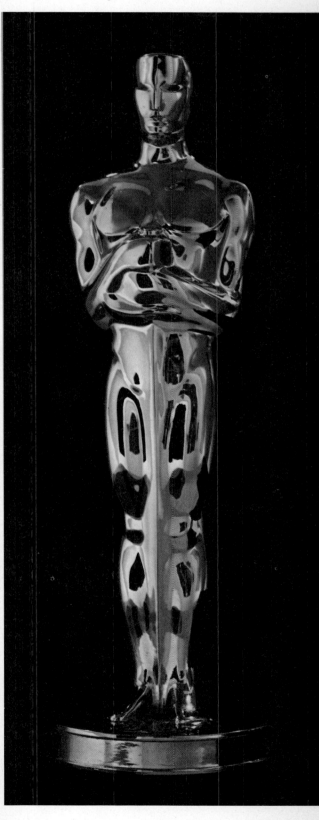

Returning home in 1940 with her Oscar, won in Gone with the Wind, Vivien Leigh puts it on her living room mantel with appropriate reverence.

The Academy Award's gold-plated statuette is 13 inches high and weighs eight pounds. At least three people claim credit for naming it Oscar.

◄ Just before the announcement of her Best Actress award for Roman Holiday (1953), Audrey Hepburn is a dramatic study of nail-chewing expectancy.

287

Louella and Hedda

Hollywood loved them as the addict loves the pusher —with a combination of fear and dependence—and their columns became a catharsis for a colony of tattlers.

It was an indication of the importance of the stars' private lives that two of Hollywood's most powerful people were not producers but gossips. Louella Parsons and Hedda Hopper, arch-rivals, wrote columns that contributed alike to the vanity and insecurity of the movie industry. Louella was the longest-reigning queen in the business; she was the first syndicated Hollywood columnist (in 1925), and at her peak her column was published in 1,200 newspapers. In 1938 Hedda challenged Lolly's monopoly. Between them, they saw to it that no show-business life was private.

Visiting a set in 1949, Louella indicates that she can bring production to a virtual halt and attract more attention than the star she came to interview.

At a 1948 benefit, Lolly shows she too can wear a silly hat, with a plume of bristles. Beside her, obscured by her own plumage, is Rosalind Russell.

After 22 years of tigerish rivalry, La Parsons and *La* Hopper (suitably hatted) try to outgrin each other facing a camera at a 1960 party.

All in from the strenuous business of helping Hedda move into her home in Beverly Hills in 1941, Cary Grant rests on a bedframe with his new neighbor.

In one of her frillier hats, Hedda gabs to LIFE about her 1963 book, a hopperful of scuttlebutt. "You can't fool an old bag like me," she said.

On occasion LIFE contrived to turn the tables on the gossips. This straight-faced "intimate"

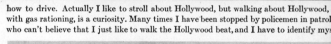

"Ginger Rogers, leaving Paramount, spots me and asks me if I want a lift. Believe it or not, I'm not going Ginger's way. But in Hollywood there'll be another celebrity along in a minute. As I patrol my beat, many celebrities have been my chauffeur, for they know I do not know how to drive. Actually I like to stroll about Hollywood, but walking about Hollywood, with gas rationing, is a curiosity. Many times I have been stopped by policemen in patrol who can't believe that I just like to walk the Hollywood beat, and I have to identify mys

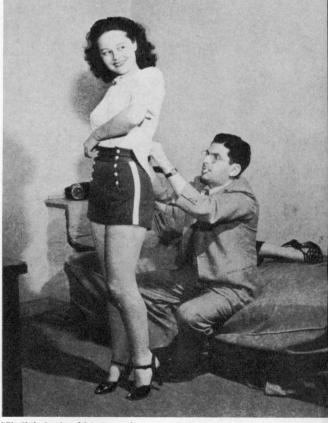

"My beat often takes me off the beaten path and for the column I not only must write about the actresses going to bed, but also how they look when they get up in the morning. One picture is more eloquent than a thousand words, and here is Rita Hayworth speaking for herself."

"The little dancing girls get around and if you're nice to them and put their names in the umn, they'll tell you what they've seen and heard while getting around. You can always di stories at musicals in rehearsal. This is Lillian Porter, from *Sweet Rosie O'Grady.* I'm no do

Life Spends a Day with Sidney Skolsky

Hollywood columnist sees stars from dawn to dark

For nearly a decade Sidney Skolsky has been Hollywood's favorite columnist. Never malicious, he is liked both by executives, who permit him to prowl through studios unescorted, and by stars, who chat with him in dressing rooms and boudoirs. Day by day he is allowed to kibitz where other intruders would be evicted on their ears. He is also Hollywood's most unusual columnist for he has no office, no automobile, no staff. He does his own leg work and writes his column wherever he finds himself at deadline. He receives his mail in Schwab's drugstore and takes telephone calls at intermediate stops on his studio and night-club rounds.

It was Skolsky who originated the term "Oscar" for the Academy statuette and the phrase "sweater girl." His column is featured by "Tintypes"—thumbnail sketches of stars—in which he usually records his subject's sleeping postures, apparel. Skolsky himself sleeps on his side, wears pajamas. Here you see him at work on a typical day. The captions are his own.

"**Maria Montez** firmly believes that a woman should look her best in her bedroom. How do I know this? She told me so, and then I went to see for myself. I was doing a tintype of Miss Montez for the column, and I had to, of course, know what she wears while she is sleeping."

Rummy is Hollywood's favorite indoor sport, and in every player's kit there is a deck ... Joan Fontaine thinks she's good (they all do); so while waiting on the set of *Jane* ... play a game with Joan in her portable dressing room. If I win, I collect in news items."

"**With the servant problem and the food problem,** you can find many of your favorite stars doing their own shopping. Judy Garland is just as confused by the points as you are. Later Judy and I visited a shop which advertises horsemeat in three grades: win, place and show."

Hope travels from his dressing room to the sound stage on a bicycle, and you'll note that ... a lift on anything. At the Academy Dinner, introducing Gary Cooper, Hope said: ... is so tall that when he wants to tie his shoelaces, he sends Skolsky down on a yo-yo.'"

"**The Irishman's Club,** composed of James Cagney, Spencer Tracy, Pat O'Brien, Frank Mc-Hugh, and others, always meets at some restaurant on Wednesday night. This Wednesday only Cagney and Tracy were in town, but I usually attend for they always have many stories to tell."

CONTINUED ON NEXT PAGE 103

Hollywood Newsreel

*The private lives of the famous were not really their own
business but belonged to the studios, the executives said
—and transgressors were often dealt with summarily.*

When a movie personality made hard news, LIFE's editors published the picture record of the event in the Newsfronts section of the magazine instead of the Entertainment section. It was not always a simple decision to make; with flocks of studio flacks at work, it was sometimes hard to tell if the story—or the pictorial situation—had been deliberately contrived to win valuable space.

Sometimes a simple encounter was news —for example, when a star-become-princess, Grace Kelly, met another distinguished Irish-American, President John F. Kennedy *(page 295)*. Certainly, movie celebrities frequently made news for less attractive reasons, usually because their real lives were so different from their reel lives. This poignant contrast between the public image and the private person was of great concern not only to the star but also to the producers and publicists whose livelihoods depended on the performer's appeal at the box office. Their guiding rule was that, as far as the public was concerned, those in the Hollywood pantheon were expected to rise above mortal sins.

For decades the image protectors cautioned any maturing sex symbol to conceal the news that he or she was a parent, on the assumption that the star's desirability in the eyes of day-dreaming fans would be diminished. The paranoia extended to peccadilloes. W. C. Fields openly brought a large Thermos of martinis with him to his dressing room every day and slaked his thirst between takes. The studio bosses publicly insisted that the container held pineapple juice—lest his fans learn that the great comedian was also a truly great drinker. In those days before the sexual revolution, the studios even blacklisted errant stars, officially or unofficially. Ingrid Bergman went off to the island of Stromboli

with Roberto Rossellini in 1949 and had his child while still married to Dr. Peter Lindstrom. Not for six years would Hollywood recognize her; in 1956 she won an Academy Award for *Anastasia.* Reprisal could come for political as well as for moral reasons: Larry Parks was blacklisted and his movie career ruined after he testified before the House Un-American Activities Committee that he had been involved with Communists.

In that era, only a few courageous and eccentric stars defied convention. Tallulah Bankhead was a rare case when she told a friend who was worrying at the prospect of being interviewed about her: "Tell him everything, dahling, only don't make me dull." Her life, Tallulah said complacently, was "as pure as the driven slush." Tallulah was ahead of her time. But the times did change: by the 1950s Marlene Dietrich could brag about her grandchild, and Elizabeth Taylor's hectic marital adventures actually turned out to be good news for the ticket sellers.

The stars and their publicists were, of course, adept at making the news in pictures, whether by pressing a part of the anatomy into the cement at Grauman's Chinese Theater or by perching on a piano being played by the Vice President of the United States *(pages 298 and 301)*. And sometimes a shot invented for a passing news premise proved to have lasting historical importance. In 1960 Eliot Elisofon asked Gloria Swanson to visit the nearly demolished Roxy Theater in New York and the resulting picture *(page 300)* said more about the bygone days of Hollywood than all the nostalgic stories of the time. And when those two veteran co-stars Mickey Rooney and Judy Garland got together for a television show, the camera eloquently conveyed the sometimes painful price of stardom.

An attentive twosome, Judy Garland and Mickey Rooney, reunited in 1963 for the opening show of Judy's TV series, watch a rehearsal from the wings.

During an official visit to the Kennedy White House in ▶
1961, Princess Grace of Monaco gazes at America's
Prince Charming in the way she once looked at Cary
Grant and Jimmy Stewart when she was Grace Kelly of
Philadelphia and a queen of the screen.

Joan Fontaine gets a hearty laugh from His Excellency
the Ambassador to the United Nations, Adlai Stevenson, at a U.N. party for diplomats and entertainers. The
joke, she told LIFE, was not repeatable.

Robert Mitchum swabs a prison corridor after a 60-day sentence on a marijuana charge. The 1948 scandal gave the industry the jitters: the studios had $5 million worth of unreleased Mitchum films.

In a Hollywood police station, Robert Walker snaps his fingers at a 1948 drunkenness charge. His life was sadly unlike his screen image of "the boy next door"; he became an alcoholic and died at 32.

Lana Turner gives a tense real-life performance as she tells a coroner's jury how her daughter, Cheryl, 14, killed Lana's lover Johnny Stompanato. When Stompanato threatened the erstwhile Sweater Girl in 1958, Cheryl stepped in to the defense of her mother with a butcher knife. She was acquitted.

The weeping widow of Douglas Fairbanks, the former Lady Sylvia Ashley, is supported by her stepson, Douglas Jr., and his wife at the swashbuckling actor's 1940 funeral. Later she married Clark Gable.

At a rehearsal of Manpower (1941), genuine fisticuffs break out after George Raft had spun Edward G. Robinson a bit too roughly. Cast in the movie as good pals, they actually detested each other.

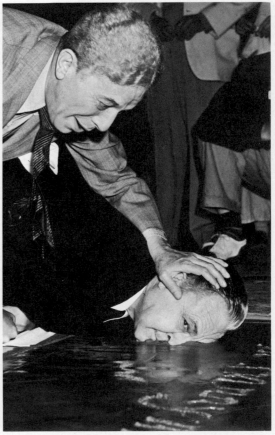

Theater owner Sid Grauman helps John Barrymore to immortalize his Great Profile in concrete in 1940 at Grauman's Chinese Theater, alongside the historic prints of Mary Pickford's dainty feet and Harold Lloyd's celebrated glasses. Barrymore's reaction: "I feel like the face on the barroom floor."

Modeling a "Mona Lisa" hairdo in 1963, Susan Strasberg hilariously alters a famous image by giving photographer Milton Greene an impulsive wink.

Kissing the startled bride, Jerry Lewis—and the bride —are swept away by the occasion at the wedding of Janet Leigh and Tony Curtis in 1951.

Carole Landis, practicing a 1940 scene in which she is to be hit by a vase, socks herself with what she thought was a "breakaway"—a prop made of brittle, easily shattered material. It turned out to be a real vase; the crocked starlet was sent home to recover.

A pugnacious Anita Ekberg emerges from her Roman villa in 1960 to threaten a pair of eager paparazzi with bow and arrow. She desisted when they gave up a roll of film—which proved to be blank.

An elegant Gloria Swanson stands in 1960 in the dismantled Roxy, the big Manhattan movie mansion that had opened 33 years earlier with a Swanson film. Photographer Eliot Elisofon's inspiration for this shot in turn inspired Hal Prince to produce the musical called Follies, set in a doomed theater.

Lauren Bacall creates a famous photograph by decorating the piano in 1945 while Vice President Harry Truman plays for servicemen in Washington.

Oliver Hardy and Stan Laurel, on a 1947 tour in Scotland, watch Sir Harry Lauder perform the "ancient Scottish rite of slaughtering green flies."

Buster Keaton drops to Toulouse-Lautrec level as he and Zsa Zsa Gabor do homage in 1959 to the Paris cabaret (and the movie) Moulin Rouge.

Epilogue

Not with a bang but a slow fade-out, the monolithic film industry distintegrated, only to collect itself again and proceed bravely with Another Opening, Another Show.

The ghost-town look of this Western street scene on the idle Paramount lot, in one of LIFE's last issues, seemed prophetic. Indeed, four years later, in 1974, Hollywood released half as many films as in 1946. But one, Paramount's The Godfather, collected $126 million, the largest gross in movie history.

At The End, Charlie Chaplin's tramp almost always lost the girl, shrugged and waddled off. By 1960, it appeared that the industry had become just such a lonely figure, abandoned by audiences with other leisure-time outlets. Some studios changed owners, others rented their properties to independent producers. M-G-M sold off its collection of props and costumes from 2,200 films, including such nostalgic relics as Andy Hardy's jalopy and the dress Judy Garland wore when she sang "Over the Rainbow" in *The Wizard of Oz*.

Now the spectacular sets were used to film TV shows. RKO was bought outright by Lucille Ball and Desi Arnaz, who had once toiled there as contract players, for their Desilu TV productions. On other lots, porn raised its head amid the TV corn. And by the end of 1972, LIFE too was gone with the wind.

But in cinema a blackout need not be Finis; it can be a promising pause in artistic progress. Chaplin's audience knew that the tramp would survive: his waddle was jaunty; his cane was twirling. The people making "movie movies" found the public would still pay to see films if they were really good. "Today a fine picture makes more than it ever did," the durable Sam Goldwyn told LIFE's Loudon Wainwright in 1959. "You have to pay three dollars and you can't get in." The end of one movie era had become the dawn of another.

THE END

Picture Credits

Credits from left to right are separated by semicolons, from top to bottom by dashes.

Introduction 4—*Peter Stackpole, TLPA—Ewing Krainan, TLPA. 5—Alfred Eisenstaedt, TLPA. 6—Gordon Parks, TLPA—Peter Stackpole—John Florea; John Morris, TLPA—Leonard McCombe—Edward Clark—Leonard McCombe. 7—Phil Stern—Ralph Crane from BS; Bob Landry—Yale Joel—Martha Holmes—Alfred Eisenstaedt.*

The Stars 9—*John R. Hamilton from Globe; Bert Stern; Leo Fuchs from Globe—MGM; Emil Schulthess from BS for Paramount Pictures; Philippe Halsman—Rex Hardy Jr.; Cornell Capa from Magnum; Philippe Halsman. 10—Culver. 12,13—No credit; Arnold Genthe, courtesy Library of Congress—MGM. 14—Homer Dickens Collection. 15—Milton H. Greene, TLPA—John Engstead; PP. 16—Phil Stern from Globe. 17—Alfred Eisenstaedt, TLPA; Walter Sanders from BS. 18—MGM—Terence Spencer; Vandamm Collection, Theater Collection, New York Public Library, Astor, Lenox and Tilden Foundations. 19—Terence Spencer. 20—Martin Munkácsi, TLPA. 21—Harry Redl, TLPA—© 1937 20th Century-Fox—Harold Trudeau, TLPA; Paramount Pictures, courtesy The Museum of Modern Art Film Stills Archive—WW—20th Century-Fox—Frank Scherschel, TLPA; 20th Century-Fox (2)—Leonard McCombe, TLPA. 22,23—Bob Landry—TLPA; Bill Ray, TLPA. 24,25—Mark Shaw; Philippe Halsman; Ettore Naldoni from BS; Philippe Halsman; Sanford H. Roth from RG; Howell Conant—Howell Conant, TLPA; Sanford H. Roth trom RG. 26—Bob Willoughby; Culver. 27—PP—Milton H. Greene, TLPA. 28—Bob Landry—Toni Frissell, TLPA; Bert Stern. 29—Mark Shaw; Toni Frissell; Allan Grant; Howell Conant for 20th Century-Fox; Paul Schutzer—Bert Stern; Roddy McDowall; Bob Willoughby; Robert Penn; Norman Parkinson—Peter Stackpole, TLPA; Philippe Halsman. 30—Roddy McDowall from Lee Gross. 31—Robert Penn—Roddy McDowall from Lee Gross; Mel Traxel for Warner Brothers. 32—Philippe Halsman. 33—Alfred Eisenstaedt, TLPA—Peter Stackpole; Philippe Halsman, TLPA. 34—Leo Fuchs from Vista. 35—Bob Landry; Harold Trudeau, TLPA—Bob Landry, TLPA. 36—Milton H. Greene; Hatami; Alfred Eisenstaedt; Michael Mauney; James B. Wood—Art Kane. 37—Carlo Bavagnoli, TLPA; Terence Spencer, TLPA—Alex Youssoupoff. 38—Sam Shaw. 40—Courtesy Lou Valentino; Culver—MGM. 41—Eve Arnold from Magnum. 42—TLPA; J. R. Eyerman, TLPA. 43—MGM. 44—Peter Stackpole, TLPA. 45—Gene Howard; Edward Carroll, TLPA—TLPA. 46—Bob Willoughby; John R. Hamilton from Globe. 47—Murray Laden—John Dominis, TLPA. 48—Paramount Pictures. 49—Culver—Paramount Pictures—Allan Grant, TLPA. 50,51—Edmund B. Gerard, TLPA—Myron Davis; John Dominis, TLPA; John Dominis—Michael Rougier. 52,53—Alfred Eisenstaedt, TLPA—MGM; John Swope; Sam Shaw; Eric Carpenter for MGM; Steve Schapiro—Alfred Eisenstaedt, TLPA. 54—Alfred Eisenstaedt, TLPA; Lisa Larsen—Sam Shaw, TLPA. 55—Steve Schapiro from Transworld Feature. 56—W. Eugene Smith, TLPA; Sanford H. Roth from RG. 57—John Swope, TLPA; Scotty Welbourne, TLPA—John Florea, TLPA. 58—Yves DeBraine, TLPA—UA. 59—Sam Shaw, TLPA—Eliot Elisofon, TLPA; Sharland, TLPA. 60—Bill Ray, TLPA; Sanford H. Roth from RG. 61—20th Century-Fox—Rank Organisation (2)—EMI; Leo Fuchs from Vista. 62—Dennis Stock from Magnum; Bill Eppridge, TLPA—John Dominis, TLPA. 63—Lawrence Schiller—Charles Moore from BS; Ralph Crane, TLPA. 64—Philippe Halsman. 66—UPI. 67—Philippe Halsman; Edward Clark; Philippe Halsman; Richard Avedon—John Bryson; Lawrence Schiller and William Read Woodfield; Lawrence Schiller; Milton H. Greene; Eve Arnold from Magnum—Tom Kelley, TLPA; André de Dienes. 68—Edmund B. Gerard, TLPA; Paramount Pictures, courtesy The Museum of Modern Art Film Stills Archive—Martin Munkácsi, TLPA. 69—J. R. Eyerman, TLPA; Bob Landry, TLPA—Peter Stackpole. 70,71—Martha Holmes, TLPA—Bill Ray, TLPA; Bill Eppridge, TLPA—Grey Villet, TLPA. 72—Philippe Halsman, TLPA; Columbia Pictures—Philippe Halsman. 73—Cyril Morange, TLPA; Loomis Dean, TLPA—Ralph Crane, TLPA. 74,75—James Whitmore; Leonard McCombe; Emil Schulthess from BS for Paramount Pictures; Alfred Eisenstaedt (4)—Alfred Eisenstaedt, TLPA (2). 76—Richard Avedon, TLPA. 78—W. Eugene Smith, TLPA. 79—© The Roy Export Company Establishment; W. Eugene Smith, TLPA—W. Eugene Smith, TLPA. 80, 81—WW; Nina Leen, TLPA—Slim Aarons, TLPA; Brown Brothers. 82—Philippe Halsman, TLPA. 83—Gjon Mili, TLPA; Leonard McCombe, TLPA; Jack Kofman for Paramount Pictures. 84,85—Paramount Pictures—Allan Grant, TLPA.*

The Buildup 87—*Philippe Halsman; Peter Stackpole—Bob Landry; Peter Stackpole. 88,89—Russell Birdwell & Associates; WW (2)—Danny Rouzer, TLPA. 90—Clockwise from upper left: TLPA; Culver; UPI; Culver; Peter Stackpole, TLPA; Sam Shaw, TLPA; The Bettmann Archive. Center: Culver. 91—Clockwise from upper left: Bob Landry; Bill Bridges, TLPA; UPI; Darlene Hammond from PP; Globe; Courtesy Lou Valentino. 92—Peter Stackpole, TLPA. 93—John Florea, TLPA. 94—Eliot Elisofon, TLPA; Loomis Dean, TLPA—Schuyler Crail, TLPA. 95—Don Ornitz from Globe. 96—Peter Stackpole—Ralph Crane from BS; Peter Stackpole, TLPA. 97—Walter Sanders, TLPA. 98—Loomis Dean, TLPA; C. A. Peterson from RG—Loomis Dean, TLPA—Loomis Dean, TLPA (2); Bob Landry, TLPA (2); Loomis Dean, TLPA. 99—Loomis Dean, TLPA—Bob Landry, TLPA; Loomis Dean, TLPA; Bob Landry, TLPA; Loomis Dean, TLPA (3). 100—Loomis Dean; Milton H. Greene; Bob Landry; John Engstead; Loomis Dean—Philippe Halsman; Berry Berenson; Phil Stern; Philippe Halsman; Don Ornitz from Globe—Philippe Halsman; John Loengard; Edward Clark; Leonard McCombe; Loomis Dean—Sam Shaw; John Raymond; John Florea; Loomis Dean; Lopert Films. 101—Loomis Dean; Peter Stackpole; John Engstead; Milton H. Greene; Philippe Halsman—Anthony Beauchamp; © Arnold Newman; Don Ornitz from Globe; John Florea; Philippe Halsman—Philippe Halsman; Francesco Scavullo; Carlo Bavagnoli; Sharland; Philippe Halsman—Ralph Crane from BS; John Florea; Allan Grant; Lawrence Schiller; Milton H. Greene. 102—Courtesy Lou Valentino—Don Ornitz from Globe (2). 103—Philippe Halsman; Bob Landry, TLPA. 104—Philippe Halsman. 105—Schuyler Crail, TLPA—Harold Trudeau, TLPA; Peter Stackpole, TLPA. 106—Loran F. Smith, TLPA. 107—Sharland, TLPA; Ralph Crane from BS (3).*

The Movies 109—*William Helburn; Gjon Mili; A. DiGiovanni for Paramount Pictures—Emmett Schoenbaum for 20th Century-Fox; Philippe Halsman; G. E. Richardson for Paramount Pictures—Mark Kauffman; Allan Grant; Eric Carpenter for MGM. 110—Gjon Mili. 112—Mel Traxel for Columbia Pictures. 113—N. R. Farbman, TLPA; Gjon Mili—MGM. 114—Courtesy Lester Glassner. 115—John Florea—Allan Grant, TLPA; RKO Radio Pictures. 116, 117—Edward Clark, TLPA; Lawrence Schiller from Globe. 118, 119—Gjon Mili; Loomis Dean, TLPA. 120, 121—Clockwise from top left: J. R. Eyerman, TLPA; MGM; Walt Disney Productions; Edward Clark, TLPA; Ralph Crane; © 1940 20th Century-Fox. Center: Zinn Arthur, TLPA. 122—Sterling Smith for Paramount Pictures; Steve Schapiro from BS. 123—Don Ornitz from Globe. 124—Walter Sanders, TLPA. 126—Albert Davis Collection, Hoblitzelle Theatre Arts Library, University of Texas—UA. 127—Clockwise from upper left: Bill Avery for Paramount Pictures; Courtesy Yakima Canutt; Movie Star News; UPI; 20th Century-Fox. Center: Paramount Pictures—The Bettmann Archive. 128—Bob Willoughby; Columbia Pic-*

tures. Both courtesy The Museum of Modern Art Film Stills Archive. 129—*UA—Allan Grant, TLPA. 130—Eve Arnold from Magnum. 131—Sherman Clark for Universal Pictures; TLPA—Bob Landry. 132—Culver. 134—Ralph Crane—Gordon Parks, TLPA. 135—John Swope, TLPA—Bob Willoughby. 136—Paramount Pictures, courtesy The Museum of Modern Art Film Stills Archive—Loran F. Smith, TLPA. 137—Terry O'Neill from Globe; UA—Walter Sanders, TLPA. 138—Allan Grant, TLPA; Eugene Cook. 139—Mack Elliott for Warner Brothers; M & A Alexander—UA, courtesy Bette Davis Collection, Boston University Libraries. 140—Janus Films—MGM; Pierluigi, TLPA. 141—Zinn Arthur, TLPA; © Richard Feiner and Company, Inc.—TLPA—Courtesy AMPAS—Contemporary Films; Walter Daran, TLPA; Janus Films. 142, 143—Ralph Crane from BS; Phil Stern from Globe; MGM, courtesy The Museum of Modern Art Film Stills Archive—Sanford H. Roth from RG. 144—William Read Woodfield from Globe; UA (3). 145—UA. 146—Bob Peterson, TLPA—TLPA; Leonard McCombe, TLPA. 147—Sharland, TLPA. 148—Steve Schapiro from Transworld Feature—Floyd McCarty, TLPA. 149—Loomis Dean, TLPA—Rank Organisation. 150—No credit—J. R. Eyerman, TLPA. 151—Edward Clark, TLPA; Federico Patellani; Franco Pinna from RG. 152—Lawrence Schiller, TLPA—Bert Cann for Paramount Pictures. 153—Columbia Pictures (2)—John Bryson, TLPA; Eve Arnold from Magnum. 154—Loomis Dean, TLPA. 156, 157—Lars Looschen, TLPA; The Bettmann Archive—Ralph Crane, TLPA; Peter Stackpole. 158—Paramount Pictures. 159—John Stewart, TLPA; PP—Allied Artists; John Swope, TLPA. 160, 161—Hal McAlpin for Samuel Goldwyn—Bob Landry, TLPA; Orlando from Globe. 162—Sam Shaw—Rank Organisation; Dennis Stock from Magnum. 163—Peter Stackpole, TLPA. 164—Edward Clark, TLPA. 166—Albert Davis Collection, Hoblitzelle Theatre Arts Library, University of Texas; © The Roy Export Company Establishment. 167—Culver—MGM; © Richard Feiner and Company, Inc. by permission of Hal Roach Studios—© 1930 20th Century-Fox. 168—Paul Dorsey—Homer Dickens Collection. 169—Allan Grant, TLPA—20th Century-Fox; Paramount Pictures. 170—Herbert K. Nolan from Globe; Leo Fuchs from Vista. 171—Leo Fuchs from Vista—Eliot Elisofon, TLPA. 172, 173—MGM. 174—Peter Stackpole, TLPA. 176, 177—J. R. Eyerman, TLPA; Sovfoto. 178—Clockwise from upper left: Culver; TLPA; Paramount Pictures, courtesy AMPAS; George Karger, TLPA; 20th Century-Fox; The Bettmann Archive; UA; Culver. Center: Culver. 179—Clockwise from upper left: Movie Star News; Culver; Andrey Andersson from BS; Ken Heyman from RG; Donald B. Keyes for UA; UA, courtesy The Wisconsin Center for Theatre Research. 180, 181—Loran F. Smith, TLPA; Larry Burrows, TLPA. 182—Walter Sanders, TLPA—Rank Organisation. 183—American Broadcasting Co. 184—20th Century-Fox—Columbia Pictures. 185—20th Century-Fox. 186—Warner Brothers. 187—Ken Danvers; British Lion Films—Samuel Goldwyn. 188, 189—Peter Stackpole, TLPA; Eric Lessing from Magnum.*

The Studio 191—*Brian Brake from RG. 192—Rex Hardy Jr., TLPA. 194, 195—Patrick Ward, TLPA; Ralph Crane, TLPA—Ralph Crane, TLPA; Mark Shaw, TLPA. 196, 197—Ralph Crane from BS—Bob Willoughby; Philippe Halsman, TLPA. 198—Dick Miller from Globe—Keystone View—20th Century-Fox. 199—Alfred Eisenstaedt, TLPA—MGM; Bob Landry, TLPA—PP. 200—Brian Brake from RG—Lennart Nilsson, TLPA—Paul Schutzer, TLPA; Terence Spencer, TLPA. 201—Franco Pinna from RG. 202—Allan Grant, TLPA; Sam Shaw, TLPA—Robert Coburn for Samuel Goldwyn. 203—J. R. Eyerman, TLPA—Alfred Eisenstaedt, TLPA; Bob Landry, TLPA. 204, 205—Walter Sanders, TLPA. 206—Bill Ray, TLPA. 208, 209—Ralph Crane from BS. 210, 211—J. R. Eyerman, TLPA—Ralph Crane, TLPA; Mark Kauffman. 212, 213—Inge Morath from Magnum. 214—Lois Weber, TLPA; Josh Weiner, TLPA—James Burke, TLPA. 215—Alan Pappe from Lee Gross—Ken Heyman from RG for 20th Century-Fox; Leonard McCombe, TLPA. 216—John Swope, TLPA. 218—John Bryson from RG. 219—Bob Willoughby—Ernst Haas. 220—Mark Kauffman; Inset, Gordon Parks, TLPA—Allan Grant, TLPA; Insets, Kenny Bell for MGM; Allan Grant, TLPA; John Launois from BS (2). 221—Bob Landry, TLPA. 222—Bob Landry, TLPA except upper left Frances Levison. 223—Bob Landry, TLPA. 224—Robert Wheeler, TLPA; John Dominis, TLPA. 225—Allan Grant, TLPA; Don Cravens, TLPA. 226—MGM. 227—Allan Grant, TLPA; WW (2). 228—Courtesy Lester Glassner. 229—MGM—Walt Disney Productions. 230—Eugene Cook, TLPA. 231—Don Ornitz from Globe (2); Allan Grant, TLPA. 232—John Florea, TLPA; Harold Trudeau, TLPA (2). 233—Harold Trudeau, TLPA. 234—No credit. 236—Ralph Crane, TLPA; UPI—WW—Leonard McCombe, TLPA (3). 237—Martha Holmes, TLPA—Leonard McCombe, TLPA (3). 238—Joe Clark, TLPA; Martha Holmes, TLPA—Hirschfeld. 239—Ralph Crane from BS—Hirschfeld. 240—American Broadcasting Co.—Jack Birns from Graphic House. 241—Whitey Schafer, TLPA; MGM—Jewel Productions, courtesy The Museum of Modern Art Film Stills Archive; MGM. 242, 243—Arthur Schatz, TLPA (2)—Walter Daran, TLPA; TLPA.*

Behind the Scenes 245—*Martin Munkácsi; Ferruzzi—Ormond Gigli; Allan Grant. 246—Bert Stern. 248—Barney Peterson, San Francisco Chronicle; Columbia Pictures, courtesy AMPAS. 249—Walter Sanders, TLPA—Alfred Eisenstaedt—Melville Jacoby, TLPA; Paramount Pictures. 250—MGM—Allan Grant, TLPA. 251—John Florea, TLPA—George Silk, TLPA. 252 through 255—Bert Stern. 256, 257—Ralph Crane, TLPA. 258—John Dominis, TLPA. 260—Yale Joel, TLPA; Bob Landry, TLPA—Ralph Crane, TLPA. 261—Bob Landry, TLPA. 262—Ivo Meldolesi from BS—Mark Kauffman, TLPA. 263—Edward Clark, TLPA; Leonard McCombe, TLPA—Edward Clark, TLPA; Alfred Eisenstaedt, TLPA. 264—Peter Stackpole, TLPA; Marie Hansen, TLPA—Dick Miller from Globe. 265—TLPA; Hans Steiner—UPI; Courtesy Dore Freeman. 266—Peter Stackpole, TLPA—TLPA; Bob Landry, TLPA. 267—Leo Fuchs from Vista; TLPA—Ralph Crane from BS; Bob Willoughby. 268—Bill Bridges, TLPA; Milton H. Greene, TLPA. 269—Alfred Eisenstaedt, TLPA; John Engstead, TLPA—Steve Schapiro from RG; John Engstead, TLPA. 270—Allan Grant, TLPA—Robert Phillips from BS; Larry Barbier Jr. from Globe—FPG. 271—Zinn Arthur, TLPA; John Bryson, TLPA (2)—Loomis Dean, TLPA; Sam Shaw from RG; UPI—20th Century-Fox. 272—Lee Johnson, TLPA; 20th Century-Fox; Ralph Crane, TLPA. 273—Steve Schapiro, TLPA—Milton H. Greene, TLPA; Sam Shaw, TLPA—TLPA; Nina Leen, TLPA. 274—Alfred Eisenstaedt. 276—Ralph Crane from BS; Peter Stackpole, TLPA. 277—Loomis Dean, TLPA; Allan Grant, TLPA. 278, 279—Bob Landry. 280, 281—John Swope, TLPA; Sam Shaw. 282—Allan Grant, TLPA; Bud Graybill for Sierra Pictures. 283—UPI—Peter Stackpole, TLPA; Ralph Crane, TLPA. 284—Irving Haberman, PM; Phil Stern, TLPA—Frank Scherschel, TLPA. 285—WW; Bud Fraker for Paramount Pictures—David E. Scherman; John Florea, TLPA. 286, 287—Peter Stackpole, TLPA; Peter Stackpole—Leigh Wiener, TLPA; Leonard McCombe, TLPA; Bill Eppridge, TLPA. 288, 289—Philippe Halsman, TLPA—Allan Grant, TLPA; Bill Ray, TLPA; Jerome Zerbe, TLPA—Bob Gomel, TLPA. 290, 291—John Florea. 292—Leigh Wiener. 294—Bob Gomel, TLPA. 295—James Atherton from UPI. 296—WW. 297—J. R. Eyerman, TLPA; George Strock, TLPA—WW. 298—Milton H. Greene, TLPA; Bob Landry, TLPA. 299—UPI; WW—Marcello Geppetti, TLPA. 300—Eliot Elisofon, TLPA. 301—Henry Wolf; UPI—Topix. 302—Henry Groskinsky, TLPA. 303—Courtesy International Museum of Photography at George Eastman House.*

Endpapers—*Hirschfeld, courtesy The Margo Feiden Galleries, New York.*

Abbreviations: AMPAS, Academy of Motion Picture Arts and Sciences; BS, Black Star; PP, Pictorial Parade; RG, Rapho Guillumette; TLPA, Time-Life Picture Agency; UA, United Artists; WW, Wide World